PRAISE

NOW Here

"This book will forever change you. Even if you're a good boss, Dom's book will make you a great one. This is a thought-provoking story and a must-read for any manager."

—CAMERON HEROLD
Founder, COO Alliance and the Invest In Your Leaders course

"Farnan's journey of tearing down personal walls and finding inner peace is captivating and inspiring. The transformation and awareness she shares in *Now Here* will challenge old leadership and birth a new way of conscious leading."

—ANGIE WISDOM
Master Certified Coach, Author, and Speaker

"Good leaders provide direction, purpose, and reason for a group or organization to follow. They also share their knowledge, wisdom, and experience with others. Their leadership becomes a calling to serve others. Dominique Farnan is a conscious leader who has risen in her business, industry, and the world. Her thoughts on conscious leadership are clear, specific, and on target in today's business and social climate."

—GERARD R. ADAMS
Serial Entrepreneur, Angel Investor, Philanthropist, and Founder of Leaders Create Leaders

"I've always admired Dominique Farnan for her unique take on what it means to walk the path to become a conscious leader. Her no-holds-barred truth telling is inspirational, and I think thousands can benefit from her successes, mistakes, and ultimately, her commitment to growth."

—EMMA ISAACS
Founder & CEO, Business Chicks

NOW Here

DOMINIQUE FARNAN

NOW

A Journey from Toxic Boss to Conscious Connector

Here

Advantage | Books

Published by Advantage, Charleston, South Carolina.
Member of Advantage Media.

ADVANTAGE is a registered trademark, and the Advantage colophon is a trademark of Advantage Media Group, Inc.

Printed in the United States of America.

10 9 8 7 6 5 4 3 2 1

ISBN: 978-1-64225-768-7 (Paperback)
ISBN: 978-1-64225-767-0 (eBook)

LCCN: 2022922449

Cover design by Gulliver Farnan.
Layout design by Analisa Smith.

This publication is designed to provide accurate and authoritative information in regard to the subject matter covered. It is sold with the understanding that the publisher is not engaged in rendering legal, accounting, or other professional services. If legal advice or other expert assistance is required, the services of a competent professional person should be sought.

Advantage Media helps busy entrepreneurs, CEOs, and leaders write and publish a book to grow their business and become the authority in their field. Advantage authors comprise an exclusive community of industry professionals, idea-makers, and thought leaders. Do you have a book idea or manuscript for consideration? We would love to hear from you at **AdvantageMedia.com**.

To Gramma Dorothy, my best friend, cheerleader, and angel
To Baxter, my beautiful son, my motivation, my teacher

CONTENTS

How I Became a Toxic Psycho Boss

To everyone on the outside, it looked like I had it all, but I was a bitter, lonely, miserable mess on the inside. I had a loving husband and a beautiful son, but my heart was hard. I had a great career and ran a successful business, but I was a toxic boss. Worst of all, I didn't feel any hope that I would be able to change because that was all I ever knew. I had been training to be like that my entire life, and the seeds had been planted very early.

At six, I fell in love with swimming. There was something about feeling weightless in the water that stuck with me and drove me to compete, so I tried out for the local Dolphins Swim Team in Lake Forest, California. After watching me struggle to make my way across the pool, I heard the coach tell my mom, "I don't think swimming is her sport. She needs more practice before she's ready."

Deflated and in tears, I begged my mom, "Can we just come back tomorrow, and you can tell her that I will try hard and practice to get better?"

My mom agreed and somehow convinced the coach to let me join the team. I made sure to hold up my end of the bargain. I listened to the coach, perfected my stroke, and poured every ounce of my energy into learning the craft. It paid off, and I was hooked—not just on swimming but also on achieving. Being the best defined my self-worth and made me feel lovable.

I brought that same focus, energy, and determination to school. Being viewed as the smartest student meant everything to me, and I became a perfectionist. I was obsessed with learning and had wonderful teachers who let me back into class during recess and lunch. They allowed me to be who I was, and so did my mom. She bought me a real-life chalkboard from a thrift store, and I turned our spare room into a classroom. I lined up a series of desks and even made lesson plans so that I could play school after coming home from real school. It's no surprise that none of the kids found that fun, so my group of friends got smaller and smaller.

As I got older, I started to identify more with my father's entrepreneurial spirit. He grew up one of seven kids, and his father worked hard to take care of the family, so he was constantly trying to escape that feeling of scarcity. It's what made him such a great provider. When I was a kid, he was a UPS driver whose route took him through South Central Los Angeles. Sometimes he worked as a long-haul truck driver and was gone for days at a time. It was a steady job with good benefits and a pension when he retired, but he was always looking for other opportunities.

I was eleven when he returned home from one of those long trips with a truckload of heavy equipment—a silk-screening machine, a six-colored press, and a dryer. It took up the entire garage. When my mom realized that he spent our last $2,500 on this ridiculous equipment, she was so irate that she almost divorced him right then, but he wasn't fazed. He told her, "I got an idea, and it's going to make us a lot of money."

That idea was to use those machines to start a side hustle printing T-shirts and uniforms for schools. He was committed and already had his business cards made and everything. That was the birth of The Uniform Man, and he pitched his idea to anyone who would listen. I was only eleven, but I spent many days, nights, and weekends helping him. He was so meticulous about the quality of our products. With my dad, everything had to be the best. I admit, there was a bit of a learning curve, and we had a couple of spats when trying to figure out how to use the equipment, but that business became successful, and soon he paid me for the work I did. That's how I bought my first car, and once I had my license, I used that car to deliver the goods to our customers. By that point, I was practically running the whole operation.

I shared that same hustler instinct as my father, but I also think his scarcity mindset was passed down to me as well. My parents always argued about money, so a part of me was afraid of being poor or unable to provide. So when my dad wouldn't give me twenty bucks to go to the mall, I didn't argue. I knew I was smart and didn't want to live under constraints or with someone telling me that I couldn't do something. I also knew that I didn't need anyone to give me anything, and the freedom to go out and get what I wanted was also under my control. I thought, *Fuck this! I need to get a job and get out of here.* That's precisely what I did, and I started working at the local pizza place.

By seventeen, we had moved to Newport Beach, California. I was on track to finish high school a semester early and had already completed several college courses. More than anything else, I felt an intense pull to become an adult and move out of my parents' house. I was able to make money at the pizza place, but with six months until I walked at graduation, I wanted to get a real job. I wanted to use my intellect, my skills, and my grit to make real money.

Robert lived across the street from us, and even though he was only ten years older than I, he worked for a thriving building products company. My father had befriended him and convinced him to hire me as a marketing intern. I spent the next six months doing literally everything the team threw my way. I made PowerPoint decks, went to trade shows, picked up laundry, and even got the company car washed. Not only did I do it all with a smile, but I also was a sponge who learned as much as I could as quickly as I could.

I only made ten bucks an hour, but it was enough for me to move out of my parents' house. I had freedom. I had roommates. And I had my sights set on my career. When graduation rolled around, the budget ran out with the marketing team, but Robert recommended that I speak with Rod, the brand-new head of HR, about continuing to work for the company in a different capacity. Rod asked if I had any interest in recruiting. *Huh? What the hell is recruiting?* That was my first thought, but of course, I didn't say that.

"Yes! Absolutely!" is what I told him. Rod hired me as long as I would continue to attend college. I was the most junior-level hire on the team and was tasked with scaling out their field sales force.

One day, Rod stopped by my cubicle and handed me a Post-it Note with a woman's name written on it. She was the candidate he wanted me to pursue and pitch one of our executive sales roles to. The only instructions I got were, "Find her and land her."

This was in the early days of the internet when there was no Google, so I had basically been tasked with finding a needle in a haystack, but I was a curious kid who liked to learn people's stories, so this was fun for me.

I knew the woman was from Dallas, so I called up one of the sales reps I had hired in that area and asked if she could send me a local phone book. It arrived a few days later, so I started smiling and dialing. Sixty people must have hung up on me before I finally found her. I was exhausted, nervous, and also surprised, but I pulled it together and explained how she had been referred to our VP of HR. He had heard amazing things about her, and we wanted to know more. She was flattered, and I put her in touch with the hiring manager.

I'll never forget the look on Rod's face when he learned that I had found her. Knowing that I had stepped up when faced with such a daunting challenge lit me up inside. I fell in love with the investigative part of the job right then. More significantly, I learned I was more capable than I realized and could make the magic happen when needed. I

I fell in love with the investigative part of the job right then. More significantly, I learned I was more capable than I realized and could make the magic happen when needed.

was hooked, and I wanted to learn as much as possible about recruiting. Luckily, I didn't have to figure it out alone. I had an amazing set of mentors who coached me and showed me the ropes. I was only seventeen, but I also acted seventeen, so when I rolled into the office in my spaghetti straps, they were the ones who told me, "You can't wear that anymore."

I spent over four years working with Rod. From that point forward, my career took off. I went from Orange County, California, to Wisconsin, Florida, Singapore, and eventually New Jersey, where I finally settled down. I worked hard, which helped me become highly successful, but the job was taking its toll on me.

I had been exposed to so many companies in so many industries, but one common denominator was that people are often irrational and lack emotional intelligence. That would lead them to project whatever they were dealing with onto me. Even if a candidate didn't accept a client's job offer, something that I had zero control over, I was still the one they took their frustrations out on. That type of stress is part of the job as a recruiter, but the problem was that I didn't know how *not* to take that personally. So I internalized everything, and it started to feel like I couldn't do anything right. That created anxiety that would manifest as a tightening in my chest and butterflies in my stomach. I was always thinking of what could go wrong and got worried every time the phone rang. I knew that if I was getting a call, shit was hitting the fan somewhere, and I would have to deal with that. I had no sense of emotional regulation and never learned that I was in control of my response because I had developed a reactive nature that started to run on autopilot. But I kept going because that was all I knew how to do, and I was also good at it.

I started my own consulting practice in 2011. That following year, I married my husband, Gulliver (yes, like *Gulliver's Travels*), and the following year, I gave birth to my son, Baxter. Pretty soon, I was making great money, but I had no downtime. It felt like I worked 24-7. I had a new family and an amazing house, but I was miserable. I lacked presence. It didn't feel like I owned my life, and I didn't know how much longer I could go on at that pace. When I told my friend Nicola how I needed a break in November 2018, she encouraged me to build on what I had and turn it into a bigger company: "You already have a small team. Why don't you train other people to service the clients, and you run the business?"

Initially, I dismissed the idea because I didn't think my clients would keep me if I wasn't the person working for them, and I had never run a business, but the more I thought about it, the more it made sense. So in 2019, I hired a team around each of my nine clients. That was officially the birth of DotConnect.

The idea behind starting my own business was to pass on the day-to-day recruiting work to my team so that I would have more time and freedom, but I ended up trading one form of burnout for another. If something wasn't delivered the way I typically did it, the clients called, texted, and emailed me to complain. When I got yelled at, I didn't manage it well, and I would freak out and go postal on my team. From the very beginning, I was a controlling micromanager. I was never trained on "how to be a people manager," so I had no clue what I was doing. I'd give somebody something to do and end up doing it myself because I thought I could do it better. I was a perfectionist, which meant my team needed to be perfect, so I pushed them as hard as I pushed myself and hovered over their shoulders to ensure they did the job right. And when they didn't, I let them hear it. I've sent a few employees running out of the office in tears for inconsequential things. It's embarrassing now, but I thought my behavior was normal then. For some reason, and I'm not sure why, my team stayed with me and was in it for the long haul.

The year 2019 was crazy, and by March of 2020, we had a solid team of thirty people. We anticipated having $10 million in revenue that year. Everyone was excited, and we were ready to go, so the leadership team flew out to my house in New Jersey for a planning session at the beginning of the month. On our last night together, we had this big dinner. Little did we know that it would be the Last Supper.

Shortly after the team left, the world shut down because of COVID-19. In a matter of days, everything imploded. It was trippy.

Suddenly client contracts ended, one right after the other. Everyone cut their budget. Those first couple of weeks were intense. I had never had to face anything like that before—nobody had. I was venturing into unknown territory, and being in New Jersey, I was in the epicenter of the pandemic. It was scary watching what was happening right on my doorstep, but there was nothing I could do but duck, cover, and try to figure out how to stay afloat. I worried about my family and our livelihood. I was worried about the business and my team. We had been working together for a couple of years and had become a family. I had brought them in and invested in them, so I wanted to preserve that. We all took pay cuts, deep pay cuts, and I took out a small SBA loan. However, I was also the breadwinner of my family, and that only intensified the pressure I felt to pay our bills. I knew on a deep level that we would bounce back, but I just didn't know when or how long I could keep this up.

In less than a month, I went from being a busy workaholic with a stacked calendar to having nothing to do. There was nowhere to go, so I puttered around the house and drank a lot more. It was getting more difficult to get out of bed, put on a fake smile, and hop on the few Zoom calls that remained on my calendar. When I didn't have to get up in the morning, I didn't. I was slowly unraveling, as I could feel my identity slipping away. After years of pressure, this was the last straw, and I cracked. I hit my breaking point and completely lost my shit. I had enough of feeling how I felt.

I didn't know what would happen in the future, but I knew I couldn't live like this anymore. Whether or not I realized it, I had been a high-functioning depressive for a long time. It took a life-altering crisis like COVID-19 for me to finally see what was wrong and admit that something needed to change. Luckily, it did. I took action and did something about it. I took my life back. Even though 2020 wasn't the year I anticipated or wanted, it proved to be the year I needed.

I know that I am not the only one who ever felt like this. At some point, we've all been overwhelmed, overworked, unhappy, or uncertain. When that happens, it's easy to lose sight of what's important and what makes you happy. That's no way to live, but despite what story you might be telling yourself right now, I also know it doesn't have to be that way. Whether you fear being toxic, stuck in a rut, not living up to your potential, or being just plain unhappy, I can promise you that there is a way out.

What follows is the story of my transformational and healing journey. This is a collection of the lessons and fundamental truths I learned along the way that now shape the way I live, work, love, and try to bring light to the world.

PART I
Live

CHAPTER 1

Change Starts from Within

While the world had descended into despair during the early weeks of the pandemic, one of the few beacons of light for me came from my friend Keven, an Orange County real estate broker I followed on Instagram. His optimism and positivity were inspiring and grounding during a time when everyone else seemed so rattled. He would often tag his coach, Angie Wisdom, and highlight what they covered in their weekly sessions.

I knew I wasn't looking for a therapist, but I had never considered a coach, so I checked out Angie's website. I liked her because she wasn't just a pure life coach. She was someone I could also bounce my business ideas off. This would be someone outside my company, even my industry, who could help me personally and professionally. Besides, Keven and I had the same vibe, so if she helped him, maybe she could help me.

I set up a call with Angie. We talked for about an hour, and I could tell immediately that we were a good match. More importantly, she had calming energy, and the whole time we talked, it felt like she was truly present in the moment. She didn't get distracted and didn't seem "salesy" or preachy like some of the other coaches I had talked to. From that first call, I was all in. "Let's go for it!" I told her.

I was optimistic, but apparently, I was the only one. Everyone I talked to seemed to fall into this hater bucket. There were a lot of eye rolls when I told people about my coach. "Why do you need a coach? Are you going to talk about your feelings now?"

Even my husband was skeptical. "Good luck with that. This chick is not gonna crack you."

I tried not to listen and went into my work with Angie with an open mind, but I also came in hot with a structured agenda about what I wanted to cover. I told her, "My life is a mess, and my marriage is a mess, but I really want to focus on work. I need to fix my business and get my team in order, and then I can deal with everything else." I was very up front, honest, and matter-of-fact—something that has never been a problem for me.

Working and making money were my identities, my drugs, my sources of motivation. I was the one who rented a boat for the day and took my friends and family out but spent the entire time working on my computer while everyone else was having fun. I'd take my family on vacation but would remain cooped up in the hotel room on the phone, taking meetings. Whether telling myself, *I have to work; I'm the CEO* or *If I don't do it, it won't get done*, my egotistical mind always had an excuse. Because I was such a workaholic and was overindexing with my career, I ostracized my family and friends. Add overconsuming alcohol, not exercising, and not getting enough sleep, and I wasn't a pleasant person to be around. Sometimes it was downright ugly.

Despite my agenda for the coaching sessions, Angie often tried to steer our work conversations back to the personal because she could see what I could not: it was all connected. During one of our early sessions, I told her I had a "hard heart." It literally felt like I had a lump of coal in my chest. After feeling like that for twenty years, I believed that nothing could soften it, but she wasn't so sure.

"What brings you joy?" she asked.

I had to laugh. "What are you talking about?"

"What makes you happy? What do you like?"

"Am I supposed to feel joy every day? That's not my life."

I had become great at putting on a show for the outside world, but there was a void on the inside. I felt disconnected from everything, especially positive emotions, never mind joy. The only emotion that came naturally to me was anger. Often, that was my instinctual reaction to so many situations. Even if I was sad or stressed, it would manifest as anger.

Angie worked with me to try and have a different reaction or way to release energy and emotion from the body. She told me, "If you feel like you need to cry, don't stop yourself from crying. Let it flow."

I quickly brushed her off.

"What's the big deal with crying?" she asked.

"That's just not my personality."

"Crying is only the movement of energy. Don't overcomplicate it or make it a big thing. Nobody's going to care or even see you. Feel your feelings, and let them come up."

She made it all sound so simple, and I'm someone who makes a big deal out of the little things, so it wasn't that simple to me. It had probably been twenty years since I cried. I thought of myself as the hard-ass boss babe. I wasn't in tune with my softer feminine energy. It was like I had tricked myself into thinking that tears were synonymous with weakness, so I took that option off the table long ago. I told

Angie that I'd try. If I felt like crying, I'd lean into my feelings and fucking cry, but I was skeptical that I would ever get to that point.

A few weeks later, I was home cleaning out old boxes collecting dust in the garage. I'm sentimental, so I keep everything, but even I know that I need to declutter occasionally. That night, I dug through these boxes and threw out letters from old high school boyfriends, but then I stumbled upon pictures, letters, and cards from my grandma. It was every important thing she had ever sent me, all in one place. I wasn't looking for it, but for whatever reason, it found me.

My grandma had died ten years earlier. The grief of that loss threw me into a tailspin. I was an emotional mess for a couple of years after that, and it still felt raw. Not only had my grandma been the nucleus of our family, but we also were kindred spirits. Our connection was rare. She was my person—my best friend. She poured everything into me. She was so supportive and affirming that she made me believe that I was capable of anything. Because of her, I grew up believing that nothing was out of my reach and that I could rise to any challenge thrown my way. I had always channeled my grandma's energy. I had used it as a guiding light and source of strength, but even that had begun to fade in recent years. Until that night.

P.S.
The reason for this letter is because you are a diamond to me and I always take care of diamonds. You are beautiful and precious.

Most Sacred
Heart of Jesus
Have mercy on
Law rence's soul

He lives in Your Heavenly Kingdom
Biography "Praise You Jesus"

Dear Lord
Mary "Our Blessed Mother"

As I sit here with a
terrible ache in my heart,
I want to write and tell you
about my loving husband:
I know you know all
about him, but I want
to put in writing any way
if it is alright.

We met at a Dance
on Christmas day, so well
I remember, that I had asked
you just before that to send
me, the one and only who would
share my life. We really
laughed because we were both
with the same last name (vigil)
I really fell for him and it
seemed that I loved him
immedietly. We dated and
we became more & more fond
of each other, and we

LOVE-NEVER-DIES

I sat down and started reading what she wrote. My grandma was always writing her feelings down. It didn't matter if it was written on the back of an old phone bill; it was incredibly beautiful. I felt grateful

17

to have found these and be able to reflect on what we had shared. I missed her so much and was so overcome with emotion that I broke down crying, but it was a happy cry. It felt really good. While I threw away just about everything else I found in those boxes that night, I took many of those letters and pictures and put them on my desk. Even today, they continue to bring me so much joy.

When I unpacked all of this with Angie, I told her how grounding it felt. Suddenly, everything she had been saying made so much sense. Crying no longer felt like the big deal it once was. I had finally debunked that story I had been telling myself for years about being a hard-ass who couldn't be softened. That all went away in a moment.

I had finally debunked that story I had been telling myself for years about being a hard-ass who couldn't be softened. That all went away in a moment.

What I didn't realize, and so many people don't realize, is that emotion doesn't go away when you push that shit down. It only accumulates, and you're going to deal with it eventually. The body keeps the score. You have to let it out. Now I cry whenever I need to. Sometimes it's from stress; at other times it's from joy. It doesn't even have to be over something as powerful or meaningful as memories of my grandma. I've cried after watching commercials. I've gotten emotional in front of my husband. He was caught off guard the first time it happened because I had been closed off for so long.

Just by crying, the door had been opened for me to feel feelings that I was scared might have been too severely blunted over the years to ever reemerge. It made me curious to see what else was in there and what else I was capable of. Most importantly, it made me realize how everything was connected and how naive I had been to start dictating how I wanted to be coached to Angie. I couldn't focus on my business first, my marriage next, and then whatever other areas I wanted to tackle. It was all connected. That became so clear at that moment because Angie made me do the work and figure it out on my own. She would pose questions and challenge me but wasn't telling me what to do or how to be. She just pointed me in a direction so that I could connect the dots myself, which made all the difference.

We all want to change, but we often look outside ourselves or point the finger at someone or something else as the reason we can't change. Very rarely do we look inward.

We all want to change, but we often look outside ourselves or point the finger at someone or something else as the reason we can't change. Very rarely do we look inward. I certainly didn't. Even when I knew something was wrong, I refused to deal with it; I blew it off, convinced myself that it didn't matter, or put the blame elsewhere. I had to take responsibility and go into this process with an open mind because nothing in my life would improve if I refused to do the inner work.

Crying was my first big breakthrough on my spiritual journey. Not only was I ready to change and become willing to do the work necessary to go deeper and heal, but I truly believed that change was possible for the first time in a long time.

If you want a new outcome, you will have to break the habit of being yourself and reinvent a new self.
—JOE DISPENZA

CHAPTER 2

Define Your Own Dark Hour

That October, I had an idea to create a membership community for women looking to learn new skills in recruiting. I envisioned it as a learning environment, like a boot camp, where I could cultivate and train women. I joined a mastermind for women looking to create these types of membership communities in their respective domains. This was also during a time when I felt a bit lonely and wanted to meet other women who ran businesses, so even though I had never joined a mastermind before, I decided to give this one a shot.

There were six women in this group, but Lindsay was the one I connected with immediately. She was a coach of high performers from the corporate world and a workaholic like me. She was also a mom with two young boys. We had a lot in common, and I thought she was smart, so I followed her immediately on Instagram and watched the videos she posted. I loved how open she was on camera. She put everything out there and was vulnerable and authentic. She always talked about the inner work she was doing and all these amazing books she read to support her journey. I found that fascinating, especially a practice she described as her "dark hour." That was the first hour of the day (which for her happened to be at 4:00 a.m.), which she took all to herself to meditate, journal, do yoga, and read books.

My first thought was, *Why on earth would she want to do that?* But her commitment to the practice was inspiring. The more I thought about it, the more I loved how she set up her morning practice. It felt like she had learned to prioritize and honor herself while balancing motherhood and work—something that seemed to have eluded me.

I knew that I needed something to improve my mental health and overall well-being. For years, even before I started my company, I'd wake up and immediately reach for my phone to sift through the millions of Slacks and emails that had piled up overnight. The minute you set up work apps like Slack on your phone, it's nonstop. My mornings often felt like an onslaught from minute one. I knew it wasn't good for me, and I certainly knew it wasn't bringing me any joy, so I tried to cut back on my own but had little success. I'd delete apps, reinstall them, and then delete them again when I realized how much time I was wasting. The phone addiction is real. It's like a drug fix, but I'd had enough of it. Lindsay helped me realize that before I plugged in to work, I needed to plug into myself, so I gave it a shot. No way in hell would I wake up at 4:00 a.m., but I started getting up earlier and took an hour to get into my zone and reconnect with what made me feel alive.

It was around this time that Angie gave me a journal. It was a hundred-day journal called "Start with You," which came with a set of questions and prompts that I made a part of my morning mindset practice. The questions were simple, such as describing my first feeling of the day. Sometimes that was all I needed to answer to get me going. I'd then write my intentions for that day and the energy I would bring to it. "I'm powerful." "I'm magnetic." "I'm the creator of my reality." It sounds simple, but committing to a practice like that felt powerful.

Slowly, a routine developed. I wish I had a name for it that was as badass as Lindsay's "dark hour," but I just called it my morning practice. Sometimes I listened to podcasts. Sometimes I'd read. There are about twenty books I love and would consider my favorites, so some mornings I just read a few pages from one of those books. That could give me an idea that I'd then write about. That's something I really enjoy doing. Since starting my morning practice, I'm on my fourth of Angie's one-hundred-day journals. I've gotten my team and even my husband to do it with me now. When I started, he was rolling his eyes, and now sometimes, he reminds me to do it in the morning.

None of this was natural at first. As an Enneagram Type 1, I have hyperachieving perfectionist tendencies, and I tend to be superhard on myself. My inner critic is extremely loud. That's helped me push myself and get shit done, but sometimes I was my own worst enemy, so when my alarm went off in the morning, I wanted to pick up my phone and look at Slack to see if there was drama going on. I wanted to read all those emails from clients I knew would trigger me. *What happened last night? Who's emailing me and yelling at us? What drama is projected at me today? Let me get into it and start reacting and feeling anxious!* A part of me craved it like it was a dopamine hit.

Yes, I would sometimes slip back into old habits. Some days, my ego took over and screamed at me, *Nah, you don't gotta do that!* On other days, I felt guilty for taking time for myself in the morning. It felt like I didn't deserve the peace and quiet because there were so many other things I felt like I needed to do, so I wouldn't do my routine. Instead, I jumped right onto my computer and started on that never-ending list of shit I had to do that day. And guess what? I'd feel all out of whack. Instead of setting intentions around the type of day I wanted to have and how I wanted to feel, I'd be reacting for the rest of the day and posting about how tired, stressed, and grumpy I was. I'd get sucked in and become a victim to the shitty day that I allowed myself to create.

It took a good three months before I made my morning practice a habit, but I learned that taking that time allowed me to be intentional about how I wanted to show up for my day. When I have a calm and peaceful morning, when I can write, read, create, reflect, and sometimes just think, that fuels all the other outputs I need to tap into for the rest of the day. I'm on fire and sometimes get my second wind later in the evening. Now I've committed to not looking at my phone for the first hour of the day. It's easier now because I've come to love this routine so much that it's softened the pull I used to have to my phone in the morning. I've even set up an area of my office with books, journals, candles, and all my morning stuff. It's like an altar.

When I started posting about this stuff, I'd get a lot of comments from people telling me that they didn't have the time, or they had kids, and they had this and that, so they couldn't do it. I get it. I have a kid, and so do a lot of people. We all have responsibilities, families, and careers, but you can find a way to make it work. Lindsay has two tiny kids who are up at the crack of dawn, but she knows how important this is to her and how it helps her be the best version of herself for that day, so she makes the time. It's the same thing with me, but it's important to remember that it doesn't have to be a full hour. It doesn't have to be any set time at all. If all I have is fifteen minutes, I take those fifteen minutes and mentally block everything else out.

Trust me; I know starting a routine can feel overwhelming, which is why it's essential to start small. If you think this will be a struggle, pick just one thing. Just one! Don't make a big deal out of it, and don't let your ego decide what's best for you; just do that one thing. Angie reminds me that all I have to do is take action. So when I feel resistance, or my inner voice is combative and trying to get me to slip back into old comfortable (yet destructive) ways, I focus on doing just one thing.

These healthy habits have a ripple effect, and you'll be surprised what can blossom from that one act. During the pandemic, I had not prioritized my health, and I was not taking care of myself, so I told Angie that I would commit to moving my body a little bit every day. It didn't have to be a big workout—I didn't even have to go to the gym. It started by going outside for a walk. Soon, I enjoyed those walks and looked forward to them because I felt good afterward. That made me want to do more, so I hired a personal trainer a few times a week. I started purposefully scheduling my workouts with my trainer at 7:00 a.m. on Mondays, Wednesdays, and Fridays, which can sometimes be difficult, but it gets me moving. It also helped to change my relationship with alcohol because when I need to get up early to work out, I try not to drink the night before and get plenty of sleep. It forces me to be intentional.

I'm not jumping out of bed every morning, and there are days where the resistance is real. I start thinking, *I should just text him and say I'm not coming*, but I fight through that. I remind myself that I've done hard things before and can continue to do hard things. When you know the tricks that the mind plays on you to protect itself, you can completely take away its power. Ever since I was a kid and faced with something difficult, I used to tell myself, "It's not forever; it's just for now." That means I know it will be hard for a little while, but that will get me to the other side, where things will be great. That's what I tell my team when we find ourselves working on demanding projects.

When you change perspective and look at these experiences in their totality, you realize it's just a drop in the bucket. Feelings are fleeting.

When I feel this resistance and take action anyway, I'm rewarded every time because it feels so good when I honor commitments to myself. The more promises I keep to myself, the more integrity and alignment I feel. After my personal training session this morning, I looked at myself in the mirror and saw how much I have physically evolved since I started. That changed my thought pattern to *You look good! You're getting fit! You're honoring yourself!* I'm back to feeling healthy. I had put off taking care of my body and exercising as I should have for several years, but now, I love doing this again. I love feeling healthy. I love starting my day with my morning practice, and I love keeping this commitment.

The ripple effect is powerful, but it has to start with you.

The ripple effect is powerful, but it has to start with you. This doesn't have to be a crazy routine that becomes a chore. If anything, it's the opposite. It's setting aside sacred time every morning to do the little things that fill you up and prepare you for the day. I've learned that part of life's beauty is that every day is a new opportunity to start fresh and wash away what you might have dealt with the day before. If you're lucky enough to wake up in the morning, you have a choice, and you can decide how you set the tone for the day.

I had joined that mastermind to create a membership community, but that plan never panned out. Part of it was just bad timing with COVID-19. I did launch a training boot camp internally at my company called Path Connect geared toward recruiting pivots, but the true benefit of that mastermind was one I never anticipated. Not only did I meet Lindsay, who has become a close friend and collaborator, but once again, when I went looking to fix my business, I also was reminded of the inner work I needed to do first. The results were a morning practice and healthy habits that have brought more peace into my life.

Change Your Thoughts; Change Your Life

One of the first things I discussed with Angie when we started working together was values, and then she had me do a very simple exercise. She gave me a sheet of paper with a long list of common values. Every-thing—from family, exercise, freedom, creativity, abundance, wealth, and time—was on the list. The idea was to give each item a ranking from one to five—five for the things that I valued the most. Some of these should have been no-brainers, but I was such a hard-ass that I couldn't bring myself to rank anything a five—not even family or health. In my mind, I had to be all in on something to rank it high, so the first time we did this exercise in June 2020, I listed my top three values:

1. Financial freedom and abundance

2. Challenge

3. Mental stimulation

In other words, I was motivated by working hard in challenging situations, likely all the time, to make money. That doesn't sound like too much fun. There were so many beautiful things on that list, such as joy, love, partnership, and family, but I picked being a workaholic who makes money in a highly stressful industry. The more I thought about it, the more it made sense. It's why I made excuses when glued to my computer every weekend instead of spending time with my husband and son. Living according to those values was taking its toll, and I was miserable.

I wasn't sure what to do about it. That's when I read the book that cracked me open: *Breaking the Habit of Being Yourself*, by Dr. Joe Dispenza. Initially, that book felt dense and bogged down with science and technical terms that I felt I missed a lot, so I had to read it twice. The second time around, it clicked for me. Each time I picked it up, I highlighted and screenshotted so many powerful quotes from it and sent those quotes to everyone I knew. When I get into something, everyone in my circle knows about it. I started buying people the book and sharing with them everything I had picked up from it. That book hit home for me, especially the part about how we all have the power to rewire our brains and change our thoughts.

Like most adults, I lived an unconscious life and never realized I had a choice in what I thought or felt. As far as I was concerned, I believed the majority of what I thought, and I was along for the ride. I became convinced that the stories I told myself about who I was and why I felt the way I felt were written in stone. Things happened, people said stuff, and I got swept up. But just because I was raised a certain way, grew up thinking a certain thing, or was told I was a specific type of person, that wasn't the way it had to be. I was learning that I wasn't an accumulation of my thoughts, my traumas, and the stories I had been telling myself. In fact, that had become my crutch, so I made a point to get rid of the crutch. I learned that I am not my thoughts.

Once I had that level of awareness, instead of repeating the stories I told myself, I chose to examine them. When I caught myself acting in a way that wasn't in line with the way I wanted to be, I worked to change that behavior by making different choices. When I found myself going down a rabbit hole of negativity, I began to pull myself out. I learned that I was much more powerful and in control than I ever realized. I could think and act differently, starting with simple self-awareness. You can choose to be angry, or you can choose to be happy. Of course, this isn't always easy at times when dealing with real issues, but each day comes with a fresh perspective, and if you choose to be present and grateful, you will reap the benefit.

> *When I caught myself acting in a way that wasn't in line with the way I wanted to be, I worked to change that behavior by making different choices.*

Learning about the brain and how it operates became particularly helpful. The human brain shifts into autopilot to conserve energy, so we find ourselves repeating the same thoughts and actions. The same is true about fear, a survival mechanism designed to keep us safe, but it doesn't mean any of those fears are real. This can't help but lead to a constrained way of thinking and being, but once you become self-aware and understand what your brain is doing and why, you learn that none of that is necessarily "you." You must get into the habit of zooming out and asking yourself why you think and act the way you do. Your essence, soul, and spirit are so much more powerful than the thoughts floating around in your brain.

The more I examined my thoughts and feelings, the more I realized I was holding myself back. I told myself I was a high-functioning depressive for a long time, but I realized I was creating my own pain. It was like I would rather be miserable, stressed out, and toxic because that's what I knew. There was comfort in that, but I was sick of it. I had reached a breaking point at which I was tired of all my shit. Who wants to be miserable? Why am I doing this to myself? Is this really fun for me? No! Of course not! It sucked! Once I realized I had the power to change that, my energy shifted. I didn't have to hold myself back. I could create joy in my life. I just had to commit to a new way of being. That was scary.

Over time, those stories I had been telling myself and the identity I had clung to lost their potency. I was in the process of telling myself a new story and creating a new identity that was much more in line with the person I wanted to become. So in January 2021, Angie and I revisited the value exercise, and the result was like night and day. This time, there were so many fives on my list. My values had evolved, and I had a new top three:

1. Peace and tranquility

2. Creativity

3. Time freedom

My family remains a priority and a value, but the way I look at it is that time freedom allows me to do more of whatever I want, including spending time with my family. The most significant change for me was that I wasn't focusing solely on work. I finally factored myself into the equation as a priority. I don't want to be on client calls all the time. I know I can create the life I want, and my choices today are anchored in those new values, so I continually seek alignment with people who match those values. Once I made that shift every-thing felt different, and it was all because of what I chose to think. I firmly believe that if you change your thoughts, you change your life—because that's what happened to me.

She once believed that the damage to her mind and heart was permanent, until she met wisdom who taught her that no pain or wound is eternal, that all can be healed, and that love can grow even in the toughest parts of her being.
—YUNG PUEBLO

The Softening of Dom Farnan

W e all carry around with us masculine and feminine energy. Your gender identity doesn't mean you carry only one type of energy. Picture that energy as two wings on your back. You need both wings to fly, so one isn't necessarily better than the other. You want a healthy mix, depending on the situation, but there are positive and toxic traits of each. Understanding those can help you find that healthy balance.

- Positive masculine energy traits: Courage, confidence, strength, discipline, focus, accountability, loyalty, action

- Positive feminine energy traits: Intuition, creativity, creation, compassion, awareness, peace, gratefulness, empathy

- Toxic masculine energy traits: Aggressiveness, bullying, greed, narcissism, arrogance, criticism, repression

- Toxic feminine energy traits: Jealousy, impatience, manipulation, unreliability, people pleasing, sabotage, shamefulness, victim mentality

After years spent tolerating toxic corporate work environments, I had grown accustomed to my more toxic masculine energy. I was dealing with corporate men the majority of my days, so it made sense that I started to act like one—even in my marriage. I was the bread-winner who took care of the bills for a long time. I no longer felt that I could just be a woman or recognize my positive feminine energy and the power that came with acknowledging myself as a woman, but it hadn't always been that way.

I remember at sixteen being beautiful inside and out, innocent, and feminine. I was a student-athlete with everything going for her, but as soon as we moved to Newport, it felt like my life became work, work, work. And then boom—I was suddenly an adult with a fucking career, so I told myself I needed to grow up quickly and be serious. That was the start of the hardening process of my personality. It accelerated when my first serious relationship ended with an ugly and painful breakup. That's when the defenses immediately came up. I decided, *OK, I'm not going to be sweet, friendly, and loving anymore.*

I was a porcupine who wouldn't let anyone get close to me ever again. I would date, but I sure as hell didn't want to have my heart broken, so I wouldn't allow myself to get into a serious relationship or fall in love. If a guy said he loved me, which was rare, I took offense and told him to leave me alone because I was not emotionally available. I unintentionally created drama in my relationships, even after meeting my husband. It almost felt like the roles were reversed in our marriage at times. When he wanted to cuddle, I was the one who was like, *Hell no!* I never made a concerted effort to be so discon-nected; I just went down a different path, and that's how I became the disconnected, hard-ass career woman. In hindsight, I know the part I played in the divide of our relationship. I made it hard to love me. I am grateful for the inner work I've done because it has allowed us to begin rewriting our relationship story.

The transformation was complete. I was emotionally closed off from the world. I had created a hard shell around my heart and buried all my feminine traits because letting anybody see that side of me would make me vulnerable. I had lost touch with that little girl, but while doing all this inner work, I couldn't help but become more self-aware of how this hard way of living was not true to myself and was not bringing me any joy. I told Angie that I wanted to be my authentic, divine, feminine self. I wanted to shed that hard-ass exterior and learn how to be softer. Instead of acting like the toxic corporate guys I worked with, I wanted to tap into my true essence and power, but I was scared. More than anything else, I was scared

This was just another story I had been telling myself that wasn't true, and I had the power to change that story.

that being in my feminine energy would impact me negatively at work. *Could I still drive the same results and be successful? Would I still be heard by my male clients and other men I worked with? Would I still be taken seriously? Would they think I was weak or dismiss me?* I had convinced myself that I needed to be this way for the company to thrive, but the more inner work I did, the more I realized this was just another story I had been telling myself that wasn't true, and I had the power to change that story.

As my relationship with myself slowly started to change, so did the way I treated my team. I no longer wanted to be the boss who always laid down the hammer. I wanted to show up firm and fair but not so demanding or demoralizing. That also included how I showed up for my husband and son. I wanted to reset the whole dynamic, but I'm so tough on everyone else because I'm tough on myself, so the softening process had to start from within, with self-love and self-compassion.

Honoring my morning practice slowly began changing my thoughts, and living life aligned with my values was a big part of that process. Equally important was learning how to let go, trust, and release control. If my instinct was to clench my fists, I had to learn to loosen my grip. That applied to both my reaction and how I approached the day. I had to learn how to be vulnerable with my heart, but I also had to learn how to be vulnerable with my business, which meant trusting the team and empowering them to show up as leaders in their own roles. Since I had been hardwired to think I always had to power through and work late, when I wasn't doing that, I felt guilty. If I wasn't filling my day up with meetings and "being productive," I felt like I wasn't doing what I was supposed to be doing. That was a trap because there was always more that I could be doing. Even though I've set my company up and hired leaders who can manage the team so I can remove myself from the day-to-day business, I couldn't help dropping into Slack and, without really thinking about it, seeing if I could rattle some cages. On more than one occasion, my team had to tell me, "Get off Slack. Leave us alone. We got this."

Of course, they were right. It's taken some time, but I've changed the way I lead and learned to loosen my grip. Still, because it's more than just a business—it's a movement I'm leading—I am the one who brings the energy to our company culture. While leading this movement is part of my identity, it's only one part of who I am today. I no longer feel the need to be the one who always worked the most and was a hard-ass on everyone. Shedding this layer of my being has been scary and uncomfortable yet empowering. I wasn't sure what I would be like in this new skin. I had been that workaholic toxic boss for so long that I didn't know who I was if I wasn't surrounded by all this drama. That was my life, and leaving that behind almost felt like a part of me was dying. It was scary. *Who am I going to be if I'm not miserable all the time?* A portion of the "new me" feels resistance to happiness being a general way of life. I'm not talking about the fake, surface-level happy facade I put on for other people, but a person who experiences genuine happiness—deep, soul-aligned happiness. It's a very vulnerable feeling, but as I've leaned into it, I've learned that many of my fears never came to fruition. In some cases, the opposite was true. Some amazing men on my team have come to me and are supportive of this new, softer, more aligned version of me. They're the same ones who laugh at my jokes and accept my masculine side, but they can appreciate the impact this new energy has on the company, and they want to help preserve and protect that.

When I've honored myself and committed to making these changes, I can see how my mood and life are just better. What really opened my eyes was how it impacted those around me— my family and team. By changing how I talk to myself, and coming from a place of deep self-love, I showed up differently for others because how you love yourself is how you love others.

> *How you love yourself is how you love others.*

The more I experience the benefits of these changes, the more natural it becomes. It silences my inner critic, making it easier for me to build intention around those practices. Honoring myself in the morning and doing all these other practices fill me with much more love and joy throughout the day while decreasing the stress and angst I would have otherwise felt; it becomes a self-perpetuating cycle. And

I know that I'm making significant progress because I never used to say things like this. You would never hear me saying I was proud of my accomplishments or how I've softened. I'd be more likely to talk shit to myself and focus only on what I could be doing better. I can't express how good it feels to be emotional and feel actual feelings again.

Now I am working on having patience and being accepting of where I'm at on the journey. It takes hard work and practice to change old thought patterns and develop new ones so that you can start thinking and acting like the person you want to be. It's exciting when you witness your own magic, and the thing about me is that everything happens at a rapid-fire pace. The minute I get into something, I become a manifesting generator—and boom! There are benefits to that, but sometimes I struggle to keep pace with myself, so I push myself harder for not being further along. When I don't see the immediate results I want, I have to remind myself that I've only just started this healing journey. I had to learn how to soften and surrender into the journey. I just have to be present and focused on what I'm doing and accept where I am in the moment. It sounds simple, but for someone like me who is always go, go, go and trying to control everything, that type of reset is another form of self-love I'm learning to practice.

Like the ocean, the native state of the feminine is to flow with great power and no single direction. The masculine builds canals, dams, and boats to unite with the power of the feminine ocean and go from point A to point B. But the feminine moves in many directions at once. The masculine chooses a single goal and moves in that direction. Like a ship cutting through a vast ocean, the masculine decides on a course and navigates the direction: the feminine energy itself is undirected but immense, like the wind and deep currents of the ocean, ever-changing, beautiful, destructive, and the source of life.

—DAVID DEIDA

Two Steps Ahead and One Step Back

I made a ton of progress during those first few months, but that didn't mean that life stopped. I was still prone to the occasional meltdown, complete with a crying and screaming fit—the kind where you have an emotional hangover the next day. They were much less frequent, but it felt like I had regressed during those moments. Like all the progress I made was an illusion, and I didn't have a handle on myself the way I thought. At times, I am embarrassed.

"Don't worry about it," Angie told me. "Sometimes on your journey, you must go back before you make that even bigger push forward. Don't be so hard on yourself and think that you need to make forward progress every day. You might go back a few steps one day and forward ten the next. But those setbacks can be a good reminder of how far you've come." Little did I know that the biggest, most life-altering setback I had ever experienced loomed on the horizon.

In 2016, I was hired to work at a big pharmaceutical company by a former boss I hadn't worked with in fifteen years. It was an excellent opportunity, but it required moving to New Jersey, so that's what we did. We bought a house in Princeton. As soon as we arrived, I worked my ass off in this tiny bedroom that had me feeling confined and uninspired. I began to question my self-worth because I was on calls all day with clients. I wondered when I would get my "big break." I needed my own space, and to me, I needed a house that was proof of my hard work. I needed to put my stake in the ground and claim it. And that's what I did.

We found the perfect house: a beautiful midcentury modern right on the water that was more amazing than anything I could have dreamed up. It was on three acres next to Princeton, where we had been staying. When you walked in the front door, the giant atrium made it feel like an estate. My son had an entire wing of the house for all his toys. And I didn't stop with the house. I wanted it all. I got the Rolex and the Porsche. Gimme, gimme, gimme—I wanted all the things. The interesting part is that even despite having all the things, you can still feel emptiness inside. When I purchased that house, it felt like I was at the pinnacle of my success, and that house and all the possessions we had in it were crucial to my identity. I needed people to walk into that house and tell me how amazing it was because if they didn't think that, it felt like a poor reflection on me.

As COVID-19 was winding down in the summer of 2021, I did a lot of traveling, and after coming down to Laguna for a working weekend in July with a friend of mine, Gulliver and I decided to bring Baxter out and spend the month of August there before returning to New Jersey at the start of September so that Baxter could start school. We had a ton of friends in Orange County. It's also where Baxter was born, so we thought it would be good for him to go back.

Moving home to California had been in my head for a while. When I first joined the company, I initially worked in the office but went remote when they renovated the campus. I didn't have an actual desk during that time, so I could go in and float around, but I mainly worked out of our home. They tried to get me back to the office, but it was such a bland, uninspiring space that I didn't go much. In the meantime, my productivity was through the roof. I had taken on all these new clients, so I could work from anywhere, but Gulli had no interest in leaving New Jersey. I loved our house, but he *loved* it on another level, which was odd since he was an Australian surfer obsessed with the ocean. I was like, "Let's move back to California. You could surf every day. Come on!" Still, he was a hard no.

I didn't think he would ever leave until that August when we visited Laguna. He started to surf more, and that's when he finally said, "Yeah, OK. You know what? I'm ready to move back to the ocean." That August, we devised a tentative plan to put the Jersey house on the market when we got home and move back to Laguna the following year. We had put a lot of money into renovating the house, so we thought we could get a reasonable price, but there wasn't a rush. The plan was for Baxter to finish the school year in New Jersey, but my mind was already racing. I started looking around and found a cool house we liked in nearby San Diego.

It felt like it would happen, so before we left Laguna for the summer, we wanted to go out with a bang on Labor Day weekend. My sister and her boyfriend, who had stayed at our New Jersey house watching our dogs while we were gone, planned to fly out to California to spend the weekend. I rented a boat, and it would be a big event. In an instant, everything changed.

Hurricane Ida hit the East Coast on September 1. Gulli had an app on his phone that got alerts about flash flood warnings as the storm made its way up to New Jersey. It didn't sound serious, so we weren't alarmed. We hardly thought about it until we got a FaceTime from my sister. They had just boarded our dogs that afternoon and were about to hop on a plane out West, but it was pouring rain. There were many gnarly storms when we lived there, so we told her to close the floodgate. What seemed like only minutes later, a giant wave crashed over the flood gate and imploded the atrium windows and blew out the downstairs windows.

I was in shock as my sister showed us the house over FaceTime. Ten and a half feet of water had flooded the entire first floor. It was almost to the ceiling and was creeping up the stairway. It looked like the upstairs hadn't been touched, but the appliances in the kitchen and the air conditioning were sparking and smoking. It felt like the whole house could explode at any minute. And it was still dumping rain!

A few weeks earlier, I had been on this spiritual journey, and everything was improving. My company was successful, the world was opening up, I was healing, and all these amazing things were happening. It was almost too easy, and then boom! My house was destroyed. My financial future was ruined. My security of having that asset was gone. All the plans I had been making in my head evaporated overnight. I had a total meltdown. Suddenly it felt like all the healing work and progress I made had vanished. I got sucked right back into a cyclone of negativity.

I didn't want to see the house, but Gulli went home a few days later. It took him a while to get a flight because they shut down Newark Airport, but the general contractor who did a lot of work on the house had arranged for a cleanup crew. When Gulli arrived, six dump trucks were outside, and workers were ripping everything out of the rotted interior. All our belongings were scattered on the lawn and covered in mud. He cherry-picked through whatever he could salvage, but they had already thrown half of our shit out. All of Baxter's stuff had been destroyed—no clothes survived, nothing. Gulli packed up a U-Haul of everything we had left, and we paid my Uncle David to drive it cross-country. I had seen the videos of the house and heard about what had happened, but I wasn't prepared when we opened that back hatch and saw everything covered in mud. We still have some of that stuff in our garage, like old paintings that need to be restored at some point. It would be another six months before I returned to New Jersey, but all those belongings in our garage remain a constant reminder of what happened.

The whole experience was surreal. It felt like somebody had died. I was clearly traumatized and didn't want to deal with anything. Still, we had to check out of the Airbnb we were staying in and were scheduled to fly home that night, but we didn't have a home to return to, so we decided to stay. I had to find a place to live and get Baxter into school there in California.

The day after the flood, I got on Zillow and started looking at houses to rent in Laguna. One thing was clear from the very beginning: this would be expensive! The housing market was in a weird place, and the process was so hard that after a few days, it looked like we would have to compromise, but somehow, I found the perfect place. It was like I had plucked out my New Jersey house and put it on a hill with an acre lot in Laguna. It was modern—very much fit my style—and it had an expansive ocean view. It was also semifurnished, which was what we needed. It was going to be a lot of money (and it's not like we had a bunch of cash sitting around after losing almost everything we owned), but I had such a firm conviction that this house was going to be the light at the end of a shitty tunnel that I hounded our real estate agent. He tried to explain how the owners already had some interest, and blah, blah, blah, but we made it work and got the house. It was only a couple of days after the storm. Gulli was still in New Jersey, so he hadn't seen it yet, but I packed up the Airbnb and moved us into this new house.

That occupied me for a couple of days, and then reality sank back. The month of October was my big cry. The first thing I did with my leadership team was cry. I told them, "Look, I need you guys to give me some air cover for the next few weeks." I still had to get my son into school. I still needed to find a car, which was way more difficult than I had imagined. During those first few weeks, I was inundated with a crazy level of admin work as I tried to set up our life in California while also running my company and keeping my sanity, but nothing was easy. The insurance paperwork was by far the worst. In October, there was a moment when our homeowners' insurance company emailed us saying that they denied all our claims, but then FEMA wouldn't offer any more help either because we had insurance. They were like, "We're not giving you anything else. Good luck!" It just wouldn't end. It was blow after blow after blow, and finally, I went ballistic. I was screaming and crying and couldn't understand why this was happening. *I'm a good person. I pay my bills on time. I pay my taxes. I'm a good human being. What the fuck?* I very much had to learn how to practice patience. I tried to have faith and not slip into a cycle of victimhood, but were there moments of victimhood? Absolutely!

As a way of suppressing my feelings and avoiding having to process them, there was a period when I drifted back into my old workaholic ways. I worked ten-, fifteen-, and sixteen-hour days and tried to create drama to feel important and take my mind off everything going on (and all the paperwork I had been putting off), but Angie helped get me back on track. She encouraged me to feel all my feelings. With her help, I could take a step back from the company and leverage my team to create space for my healing. If that meant I needed to go book myself a hotel room to cry, then that's what I needed to do.

It took eight weeks before I finally turned a corner and realized that I couldn't stay in that negative energy anymore. What was weird was that suddenly the whole experience felt kind of freeing. We had just talked about selling that house and moving back to California, but the thought of packing up an entire forty-four-hundred-square-foot house and hauling all that shit we had accumulated over the years felt overwhelming. Slowly, my perspective began to shift. Now that time has passed, I look back on the hurricane not as a tragedy but as a character-defining moment.

That house represented my success. It was stripped away in an instant, and none of that changed my self-worth or the impact I could have on the world. That experience forced me to reevaluate what's truly important. I realized that I feel solid. I feel content. I feel good about myself and who I am. Today, I don't want the big fancy house or need it to show the rest of the world I made it. Just the thought of it makes me feel like I'll have to work till I'm a hundred to pay it off. The pull toward the material lifestyle has evaporated, and I feel so much lighter and happier because of it. I don't wish that experience upon anyone, and I would never want to live through anything like that again, but it was a lesson.

That disaster put things in perspective in a way that very little else could. Before, when something bad happened, I would be more likely to play the victim, find an excuse, or blame someone else. Now, I don't spend my time doing any of that. I can look back and laugh at how I would blow so many foolish things way out of proportion. When you experience a natural disaster, or what the insurance industry would call "an act of God," you're forced to sit with that and understand there was nothing you could have done to prevent it. No plan could have changed anything. It made me realize how little we are in control, and for someone who was all about control, I felt it was both scary and liberating at the same time. The only thing I could control was my response, and everything else, be it a minor setback or a major catastrophe, had been a part of the plan before I ever knew what the plan was.

It made me realize how little we are in control, and for someone who was all about control, I felt it was both scary and liberating at the same time. The only thing I could control was my response.

I feel thankful that the hurricane happened when it did because if I hadn't had Angie and all that healing work under my belt, I would be in a very different position today, personally and with my family. I embodied what I had learned along the way to be resilient for Gulli and Baxter and for my team because it wasn't only about me. They were going through their own struggles.

One of the most profound things Angie said was that it's normal for someone to go backward before they're about to transcend to another level of healing. I didn't realize it then, but that moment was right around the corner.

When we meet real tragedy in life, we can react in two ways—either by losing hope and falling into self-destructive habits or by using the challenge to find our inner strength.
—DALAI LAMA XIV

Stepping Out of My Comfort Zone

I had followed Gerard Adams on Instagram for a while before the pandemic. He was an entrepreneur and coach who had run various masterminds and business leader forums. During the COVID-19 pandemic, his focus pivoted, and he started a conscious leaders' mastermind, so I signed up for the second cohort in February 2021. It was one of the best decisions I ever made. The group created a very "Come as you are, and we will love and accept you" kind of vibe that resonated with me. It was unlike anything I had ever experienced before.

Gerard and I were around the same age and had similar values. Having exited a couple of companies, he was also impressive business-wise yet was so down-to-earth and humble. We had a lot in common and even shared a similar story: he was close with his grandma before losing her, so I felt an immediate connection with him. He was humble and spiritual and enjoyed life. He brought such incredible energy to everything, which made him so calming to be around. He quickly became one of my favorite human beings whom I ever had the honor of knowing, and he opened my eyes to the spiritual realm and all the possibilities at my doorstep. He changed my life.

The more I came to know Gerard, the more he challenged and inspired me to step out of my comfort zone and start doing things I hadn't previously done. I always loved to travel, but all of my trips had been partying trips with my girlfriends. That started to change when I met Gerard and began my conscious journey. The first trip I took with the group was to Tulum, and it was a spiritual healing retreat. I had no idea what that meant. I was dead sober the entire time. We did breathwork, a temescal to sweat out our toxins, and a ton of other deep healing work I had never done before. It was so different for me, but I felt called to do these different things.

After Tulum, I traveled to Costa Rica with my friend Yerlin, where I had my first experience with plant medicine and found myself hiking and jumping off waterfalls. This was a giant leap for me because I have a lot of fear, but whenever I felt afraid of something and did it anyway, I was quieting that inner critic and overcoming my impostor syndrome. With every fear overcome, I could take back a little bit more of my power. I did that enough, so it started to feel like I could accomplish anything. That left me craving and seeking another way to step out of my comfort zone.

Whenever I felt afraid of something and did it anyway, I was quieting that inner critic and overcoming my impostor syndrome.

If I can feel like that, absolutely anybody can. Talk to any of my friends, and they will tell you that my ideal trip is doing something bougie, like going to the South of France to sit on the beach with champagne, but after stepping out of my comfort zone, I was hooked. All this brand-new stuff that I was discovering about myself was fun for me. Gulli would joke and call me the "fun police" because while his idea of fun was being the life of the party, I suddenly wanted to be healing the depths of my soul with breathwork and ecstatic dance. I love that shit now. Give me more of that!

I started traveling a lot, going to places and doing things that I would never have considered even just a year earlier, but when Yerlin invited me to join her on a trip to Antarctica, I slept on it for a minute. My first instinct was that it was too extreme a destination, where I would be cut off from everything. Plus, I hate the cold, but the more I thought about it, the more it appealed to me. I wanted to go somewhere different, be somewhere new, and do something that was the total opposite of me while completely disconnecting from any device. Suddenly, I had to go on this trip. Nobody believed me when I told my team I was going to Antarctica, but I was committed.

First, we flew to Santiago, Chile, and then down to Punta Arenas, Chile, where we boarded a boat for one week that took us across the Drake Passage to Antarctica. I was completely off the grid. I wasn't in touch with my team, and for the first time, that felt OK. That gave me the feeling of freedom and helped to reinforce the idea that the weight of the world was not resting on my shoulders. I became comfortable with the idea that I could take a break and do the things I wanted. It allowed me to enjoy myself and not feel guilty.

Down in Antarctica, all you see are massive glaciers. There is nothing else there—no houses or anything. It's just this expansive, pristine landscape that is entirely untouched. The horizon looks like it goes on forever. You can't see the end of it, and when you witness something like that, it can't help but do something to your brain and change how you think and view the world. It made me feel so small but in a good way. It made me think my dreams and the impact I could make on the world that could be more significant. It was no longer about just me and my team. I started asking myself what we could do to create bigger ripples.

I started asking myself what we could do to create bigger ripples.

Antarctica has this mythic weight. It resides in the collective unconscious of so many people, and it makes this huge impact, just like outer space. It's like going to the moon.
—JON KRAKAUER

When I returned home from Antarctica, I felt so expansive and wanted to get my message out about bringing consciousness to corporate. I wanted to change how people hire their teams and build their companies. When I began my journey a few months earlier, I had this idea in the back of my head, but it felt more like a long shot or something that wasn't realistic. It was now at the front of my mind, and I was 100 percent aligned with that vision. I knew that was why I was here and what made me different. I've always recognized that how I do my job and show up is totally different from anyone I've ever worked with, but I finally had a strong conviction to put a new stake in the ground and fully commit to this idea. Instead of trying to do it in a low-key way or thinking small, I was all in. I would verbalize and share it with the world because it needed to happen.

Everything made sense. I had a purpose for myself, my company, career, future state, and impact. Without a doubt, I would never have arrived at this place had it not been for those recent experiences and breaking out of the confining shell that once defined me. When you step out of your comfort zone and challenge yourself, it can't help but give birth to a different way of thinking. That leads to change and innovation. I can now see how naive I had been at the beginning of this healing journey to think that I

Everything made sense. I had a purpose for myself, my company, career, future state, and impact.

could simply fix my business and then work on myself. All this deep healing work certainly wasn't complete. That will always be a work in progress, but I had laid the foundation, so I could continue to grow. I finally had the vision to look at my business from a fresh perspective.

Discomfort brings engagement and change. Discomfort means you're doing something that others were unlikely to do because they're hiding out in the comfortable zone. When your uncomfortable actions lead to success, the organization rewards you and brings you back for more.
—SETH GODIN

PART II
Work

CHAPTER 7

A New Vision

Despite my frustration with the industry and my business, I still loved my job. That hadn't changed since I had first stumbled upon recruiting and had fallen in love with it at seventeen. There were moments when I could see myself doing something else and taking a position outside of recruiting. At one point, I looked at my in-laws, who made high-end sourdough bread at their bakery in Australia, and a part of me wanted to leave everything behind and do something like that. It was liberating and fun to think about, but I didn't ever have a passion for anything else like I did recruiting, so I never had a good reason to leave. I enjoyed learning how companies were built and the different functions and types of jobs within those companies. As recruiters, we're on the front line. We're the first contact with the talent that a company needs to build its business.

Once I started building my own business, I developed a whole new appreciation for what we do. That experience changed how I approached the job, specifically the rush to get everything done. It can be frustrating when a hiring manager takes forever to make decisions, but I learned the hard way why that's sometimes necessary. I rushed the process, misfired, and brought the wrong people on board, only to have the situation blow up, which cost us a lot more money to fix. When you aren't intentional and mindful about how you recruit, it can kill the morale within your company. It's in my best interest as a recruiter to get things done fast, but having been on the other side of that equation and having made some of those mistakes, I've learned how to balance those competing demands so that our company and the client can both come out ahead.

I returned from Antarctica with a new vision to bring consciousness to corporate. It required looking at every facet of the company and rethinking how we did things.

I may have loved my job, but for a long time, something was missing, and that final piece of the puzzle finally fell into place when I returned from Antarctica with a new vision to bring consciousness to corporate. It required looking at every facet of the company and rethinking how we did things. It started with our team because we needed people with a similar vision if they were going to follow through and take us to the next level.

I get that what I was trying to do wasn't everyone's thing, but I wanted to create a company at which everyone was in complete alignment and their energy channeled in the same direction. Unfortunately, that meant some people had to leave, including one of the first people I ever hired and taught recruiting—this was before the DotConnect team was even a thing. One of our clients recruited her, and I supported her decision to take the job because it was a better fit. I wish her and everyone we parted ways with the best, but everyone we kept needed to be in complete alignment.

The next step was to reexamine our company values. When we first created our website in early 2019, I sat down with everyone, and together, we came up with a series of values. We had a small group of people, but they were smart, and I wanted their input, so we put time into this exercise. It went through a couple different iterations, but we finally settled on three core sets of values:

1. Drive and curiosity

2. Creativity and innovation

3. Ownership and delivery

By the time I returned from Antarctica, I was personally undergoing a massive shift, and my values had already started to change. It was only fitting that my professional values evolved as well, so we revisited our company values during our first quarterly meeting in late January. Once again, it was a process. We came up with a list, tried living with that list for a couple of months, and then officially pinned down this new list of five values in April.

1. Mindfulness

2. Willingness to help

3. Driven by a growth mindset

4. Ownership and delivery

5. Having fun

It felt like many people on my team were side-eyeing me. *Is she really into all this healing stuff, or is this just another bunch of bullshit?* They didn't all believe me at first, so some were defensive and resistant. Some just flat-out didn't think any of this was going to happen. *Fun? Sure. You intentionally want to have fun here?* I don't blame them because even though I could joke with them about ridiculous things, they all still knew me as the super serious, control freak who was a perfectionist regarding the company and our jobs. It didn't make much sense to them, so I get it, but whether they all realized it or not, I was committed, and if I expected anyone else to change, it needed to start with me.

> *I was committed, and if I expected anyone else to change, it needed to start with me.*

It's one thing to speak about the values or post inspiring messages on Instagram, but it's another to truly live the change. I had to embody it. That meant showing up differently than I had before because I couldn't say that I was trying to instill all these new values and continue to go postal on my team for little shit. I had to be more mindful, which meant that I had to stop, think, and maybe even take a walk to chill out before I reacted so that I could approach that situation from a healthier emotional place. If the team was going to change, they needed to feel that I was changing, and that was something I couldn't fake. The best way I knew how to do that was to open myself up.

I used to be terrified of failure, and it trickled down through so many different things I did. When we started the company, I didn't want to create a website because I was scared that we would look bad if we didn't get any work, so I didn't want anyone to know that we tried. I just wanted everyone to think I was the best recruiter ever. Now I don't even use the word *failure*. When things don't go my way, I look at it all as part of the plan. I put all my shit out there because it's just part of the journey. When you show up as your true, authentic self—flaws, failures, and all—and you're honest with people, they resonate with that. So I talked openly about my depression and the experiences that had inspired my healing journey. That was the best thing I could have done because being transparent and authentic gave my team permission to do the same. After that, many of them felt comfortable sharing similar experiences with me.

These values weren't only for the leaders. We wanted them reflected on all levels and in the hires we made, so we vetted our team to ensure everyone was indeed in alignment, but it wasn't hard to figure out; I could tell simply by how people acted. One dead giveaway was whether they showed up to the one company-wide meeting or not. We only have one a month, so I'm not asking a lot there, but those people who didn't make an appearance were definitely on my radar. I wanted to say, "Do you really want to be here? If not, don't take up space for those who are on board and want to make an impact." But I also knew that I needed to have patience.

Becoming grounded in these values took some time. We hold monthly all-hands meetings, and when I tried to talk about these new values during one of those meetings, there were crickets. Nobody could think of one. That meant we had an opportunity from a leadership standpoint, so we set out to change our vocabulary and explain what behaviors reflected our values. They say it takes a minimum of seven times for an adult to hear something before it sinks into their brain, and they can retain all the data around that point, so we continued hammering this home.

By making a conscious effort to ground everything I do in these values, I can lead and live by example.

I have a Post-it attached to my computer that I'm looking at right now listing all five of these values. By making a conscious effort to ground everything I do in these values, I can lead and live by example. Pretty soon, the team followed suit. Now, when we talk about our values during our all-hands meeting, everyone chimes in and has something to add. It may seem ridiculous to the outside world, but it's important for us.

We will learn that though we think big, we must act and live small in order to accomplish what we seek.
—RYAN HOLLADAY

Not everything changed when I returned from Antarctica. It wasn't a complete overhaul of what we believed in and how we did things because we were still doing the same job for the same clients. Values like ownership and delivery remained the same. And we always looked for people with a growth mindset, even at the junior level, because if you don't have a growth mindset, you're not going to do well with us. During the first year of the job, there's a lot to learn, and you're constantly having new things thrown at you all day, so you must be interested in learning. If you're stuck in your ways, you can't grow.

When it came to the new values, most required a simple shift in perspective. Adhering to "willingness to help" sounds like a no-brainer, but it's often overlooked. This is a business where you must get used to hearing, "No!" Most of the feedback we get from candidates, hiring managers, and companies is negative. It's "I don't like that person" or "I don't want that job" all day. That makes it very easy to be negative and feel defeated, but in those situations, we want our team to do the opposite so that they can devise a good solution for everyone. So, when you get that negative feedback, and it appears like everything you worked on just blew up, you flip the script. "OK, so you don't like this job; how about this one?" "You don't want this client? Help us better understand what you're looking for." Sometimes that's all it takes to turn a negative situation positive.

Simple changes like that can be infectious in unanticipated ways. I can't think of a bigger compliment or a sign that we're on the right track than when I hear one of my newer team members say they've never worked in an environment where everyone goes out of their way to help each other. That's so unlike most people's experience in corporate, where they wish you luck and release you out into the wild. I worked in corporate for a long time and felt like I was on an island. I want a company where we're all in this together, for the good and the bad, not everyone for themselves. That all starts by lightening up.

In the scheme of life, we understand that work is just one aspect of it, so why do we let it bring us to our knees and ruin our days sometimes?

Look, I know recruiting can be a thankless job at times, so why not make it fun? And why not make that a company value? I'm not talking about crying and breathwork. That may be fun for me, but it's not everyone's bag. When I say fun in this context, I'm talking about not taking the job so seriously. Let's put things into perspective. We aren't saving lives or trying to put people on Mars. In the scheme of life, we understand that work is just one aspect of it, so why do we let it bring us to our knees and ruin our days sometimes?

I think back to when I started my career—how seriously I took everything and how hard I was on myself. My perfectionist ways weighed me down and left me operating from a place that was not good for anyone. Now I see how my junior recruiters can get down on themselves when they get yelled at or have to deal with other people's projections. They get flustered and sidetracked and can easily let another person's negative energy make them anxious. They take it hard, hold onto it, and let it eat them up inside. It's just unhealthy, so I don't want them to go through the same thing I did because much of that negativity is just noise. Many things in life are much more important, so I strive to make work a little lighter. As Angie would say, "You're the one in charge of deciding whether things are light or heavy." And she's right. I used to say things felt heavy, but that was my choice, whether I realized it or not. I'm the one who decides the weight of the items that come across my desk every day. It doesn't have to be heavy if we don't make it so, but that doesn't mean we aren't serious about what we do.

At DotConnect, we take the job we do very seriously. That's not something that will ever change, so our team members know they must perform. What I no longer want our team to take seriously are the outrageous demands, the politics, and the drama. So when one of my clients calls me up to yell that we wasted his time because we sent him "the worst candidate ever" (a real quote), I take a step back and assess the situation from a place of calm and don't allow myself to get angry or defensive.

I don't catastrophize because I can put things in perspective and focus on what's truly important: helping people find their dream jobs.

"I'm sorry we wasted ten minutes of your time. Thank you for your feedback. We're going to use that to improve our process for you. It sounds like you need to talk to my recruiter so that you two can get on the same page. Let's figure that out."

That's it. Old me would have made it a big thing and taken it out on my team, but today, I try hard not to allow any of the meltdowns, fights, and stress into my energetic field. I don't catastrophize because I can put things in perspective and focus on what's truly important: helping people find their dream jobs. It may have taken me almost twenty years, but I've finally learned that there is nothing that isn't fixable in our world. Even if it's the client's worst nightmare, we'll figure it out and find a way to move forward. We always do.

This new approach felt unnatural at first, but as with anything, the more I practiced it, the better I got, but I still slip up and revert back to old habits. I catch myself sometimes being defensive instead of curious, but that's OK. It will happen, and when it does, I center myself, get calm, and try again. This process isn't about changing overnight or getting things right the first time. It's a long game, and you win that game through self-awareness. Becoming more aware is half the battle because when you closely examine your thoughts and emotions, you can better recognize when you're being unfair to yourself. That makes it easier to regroup and realign yourself with the values you want to represent so that you can show up differently.

These new values are at the forefront of everything we do, from client meetings to sales discovery calls. If we're going to bring consciousness to corporate, we need to lead and live by example. However, I couldn't just set the tone and hope my team followed suit. There was one essential leadership quality I had overlooked in the past and needed to embody. If we were going to succeed and bring this vision to fruition, it was my responsibility to grow the skills and confidence of my team.

Perfectionism is not the same thing as striving to be your best. Perfectionism is the belief that if we live perfect, look perfect, and act perfect, we can minimize or avoid the pain of blame, judgment, and shame. It's a shield. It's a twenty-ton shield that we lug around thinking it will protect us when, in fact, it's the thing that's really preventing us from flight.
—BRENÉ BROWN

CHAPTER 8

Investing in the Team

I n 2011, I formed DotConnect on paper, but I didn't have a team or anyone working for me. By 2018, I had about nine clients, so I took on my friend Erica and a couple of other part-timers whom I paid out of pocket as they moonlighted for me, but I was the one who was face-to-face with the client. They only knew and interacted with me. I didn't want it any other way, but if I expected the company to grow, that could only last so long because I would need help, and pretty soon, I exceeded my bandwidth.

My biggest client kept feeding me more work, which stretched what I could do as an individual to the limit. Finally, I threw up my hands and told them, "I'm just one person. I can't take on all this, but I have a team." That was news to them, so I proposed a solution. "We can renegotiate our contract, and I can bring in my team so that we can take on more work for you." They were fine with it, so I figured my other clients would be as well. I went to them and made the same deal. That's how it started.

Slowly, I brought on more people and trained them. At first, they were people close to me and already in my network, such as family, friends, and relatives. I wasn't paying them very much, but they saw what I had built and wanted to learn. I knew how lucrative the job could be when it's done well, and I enjoyed teaching them a skill that could transform their lives. Besides, it's not rocket science. That year, I brought on twenty-five people, and we were still growing, but there was a downside.

Since I was hiring people close to me, some took advantage of that by taking the money and not doing the work. I had no clue until I got calls from clients saying they hadn't heard from so-and-so in weeks. I'd follow up, and sure enough, so-and-so had taken the paycheck and went off to Bali. Not good!

The story I told myself was that those team members never saw me as a boss or respected me as a leader. When you start working with friends, the dynamic can change. You can grow apart, or you can grow together. Some even try to move in on what you've created. I tolerated a lot of mansplaining, but it wasn't just the men. I've had women try to tell me how to run my company because they assumed I didn't know what I was doing. Impostor syndrome was inevitable, and I couldn't help but wonder if they had a point. *Maybe I don't have any business trying to do this.* That thinking bled over into my management style and planted the toxic seed that would spread and rot the company from the inside out.

I felt a constant need to prove myself and my worth, so I tried to do as much as possible on my own. It was an instinct I had developed early. I had been on teams throughout my career where it felt like I was the only one who contributed. I would try to mentor and inspire, and sometimes others picked up the slack, but after a few weeks, it was back to how it was before. I just decided to do what needed to be done because it was the only way it would get done. Maybe that was true, and maybe it wasn't, but I sure as hell believed that, so when I was in charge, it was hardwired in me to take the lead. I didn't want to delegate anything or ask anything of my team that I couldn't do on my own. The consequences of not taking action have always been a strong motivator.

By 2019, I was very much in the trenches with my team. It wasn't a normal work relationship for many of them. It had more of a start-up vibe, as they were friends who basically lived at my house 24-7 as we collectively worked around the clock. And it was not the healthiest environment—at times, it was a downright abusive relationship. They say you're often meanest to the people you're closest to, and that's how I was

> *They say you're often meanest to the people you're closest to, and that's how I was treating my team.*

treating my team. I don't know how much longer we could have gone on that way, but we'll never know because everything changed when the pandemic hit in March 2020.

Our team went from twenty-five people down to fifteen and then dropped below twelve because we didn't have any work. I dipped into the little savings I had so that I could continue paying everyone, but since it's easier for one recruiter to get a job compared to me trying to keep a dozen people employed, I encouraged them to apply for whatever jobs they could get on their own. Some of them were able to find side projects, but I made sure to stay connected to the core group so that if (and when) one of those bigger projects came in, I could pull us back together. Meanwhile, I waited and slowly started to unravel.

With the company in limbo, I felt a deep longing to change something, but I didn't know what. I sought answers everywhere. I asked Angie to help me fix my business and joined masterminds to surround myself with female business owners, hoping that I'd pick up on some secrets to success that I could leverage. During these masterminds, the other women would vent about their teams and all the

After listening to how these women spoke about their team, it hit me. The problem wasn't their teams; it was them! And I was one of them!

problems they had with their people. At first, it felt easy to commiserate with other leaders who talked the same way because I was that leader who used to vent and get frustrated at everyone else. But after listening to how these women spoke about their team, it hit me. The problem wasn't their teams; it was them! And I was one of them! I was very hard on myself, but when things went wrong, I would take it out and blame my team without understanding that the failings of my team were my fault. *Whoa!* That landed hard.

Zoom out, and the team is a reflection of their leader. I mean, seriously. How can all fifteen people on your team be negative? Hello! You set the vibe with your energy, and that trickles down throughout your team. If you're a toxic asshole, chances are that your team will be as well—if they even stick around. Sometimes you don't even know you're toxic. That was me. I had no self-awareness. I just thought "how I was" was normal.

This revelation coincided with the awakening I was going through and the healing work I had been doing. I continued to work on myself until the jobs slowly started to roll back in at the end of 2020. We landed a couple decent-sized projects before things began to normalize in 2021. Pretty soon, my bigger clients were hitting me up, and they needed huge teams of recruiters because that's when companies really started to scale. Not only did we bring most of the original team members back, but we also consistently added ten new people a month for the rest of the year until we had about one hundred team members scattered all over the world. About thirty of them are located near me in Southern California. I have an East Coast team whom I see when I travel out there, a few satellite people near Seattle, and an international team in South Africa. I made Erica, one of the first people I ever hired, my COO, and now four people report directly to her. The organization took on a completely different shape, but the infrastructure wasn't the biggest change—it was how I approached leadership.

> *The organization took on a completely different shape, but the infrastructure wasn't the biggest change—it was how I approached leadership.*

I learned a lot during the pandemic. I had a different perspective as the world started to open up, and this time, I was committed to being a different kind of people manager. Sitting among the stack of books I read that year is *The 15 Commitments of Conscious Leadership*, by Jim Detmer, Diana Chapman, and Kaley Klemp. The first commitment is taking full responsibility for the circumstances of your life—your physical, emotional, mental, and spiritual well-being. One of the many lessons I took from this book is that a true leader takes ownership, and that's what I started doing.

I took responsibility for growing the skills and confidence of my team, and so did the rest of our leadership team. We made sure to actually say those words so that our leaders could step into that posture and feel empowered. It required having honest conversations and opening up lines of communication to create a culture of accountability in which people weren't always looking to pass the buck. It's what's best for the team and also the company because having a confident and competent team makes any leader's job easier. And for help making this cultural shift, I turned to the person who had helped me grow so much over the past year.

Angie ran a ten-week group coaching program for both companies and individuals. My husband went through it, my uncle went through it, and my sister went through it, and after seeing how much Angie had changed my life for the better, I offered my leadership team the same opportunity—I'd pay for it, of course. That was never something provided to me during my years in corporate, even by my best bosses, so I felt it was a way I could give something back to my team while getting us all on the same page in terms of values and vision.

We started with the leaders and then encouraged emerging leaders and high-potential people to take it as well; about fifteen people have taken the course so far. And since different people start at different times, they aren't always in the same group or even with other Dot-Connect people. That can be good because not everyone wants to be vulnerable and lay all their shit out there for their colleagues to see. It's easy to put up barriers in that situation, but for most, it's not a problem. We are a close-knit group that has already been through a lot together, so everyone is supportive. We build on that and have reached a point where we can talk without judgment and feel safe to share stories and connect on a deeper level. That inspired many of our team members to take action toward their own healing.

One of the best ways I've learned to help the company and my team was by recognizing my strengths and development opportunities. Sometimes that means getting out of my own way by delegating the tasks that I'm not amazing at. What would those be? Let me put it this way: I love mentoring people. I love teaching people, and I still consider myself a student, so I look at those relationships as a two-way street or a collaboration. What I don't like, and what I'd be lying to myself if I said I was good at, is the day-to-day management of people. I'm probably not supposed to admit that in a book like this, but I think of myself as a leader, not a manager.

When I was young, I was a manager's dream. You tell me to do something once, and I'd do it right every time and make you look good because I was a quick study and got shit done. The problem is that when I manage other people, that's what I've come to expect, and there aren't many people like that. I was never a person who needed that, so I never became good at providing that type of direction. It's something I'm working hard to improve upon, but it wouldn't be in my team's best interest if I tried to take on that role. Some people are good at this, and I'm not one of them, but I have one on my team.

Erica is a phenomenal people manager, so day-to-day performance and team management are the roles she's embraced. She leans into her strengths so that I can lean into mine, and the company is better off because of it. Selfishly, that allows me to play good cop more often—a nice change of pace and a role better suited to my current path. It's nice to be the one who is fun, friendly, and full of energy for a change. Today, I can say without hesitation that I am completely confident in my team's ability, and I back them 100 percent.

> *Today, I can say without hesitation that I am completely confident in my team's ability, and I back them 100 percent.*

Support for my team comes in all sizes, and it wasn't just about healing work. Sometimes the best thing I could do for my team was give them a day off when needed. I don't want to force people to go on a retreat and do a bunch of team-building exercises that they all hate. Who does that benefit, and does it really make anyone more invested in what we're trying to do? Instead, we surveyed the team to determine what they wanted to do. This allowed them to be more intentional with the activities we created, and we've stumbled upon some creative outlets. One time we did a Zoom magic show. Another time we did this Bob Ross–style painting thing where we shipped painting kits to those who wanted to participate so that we could all do it together on Zoom. Other times we've done a beach cleanup and then gone to my house for a barbecue. We even started up a book club.

Our team may be scattered all over the world, but I encourage everyone to meet up together as much as possible. That's a lot easier for those close to me in Southern California, but for the others, we've given them the budget to get together and go golfing, host a barbecue, or just hang out and get lunch. We have them take a couple of photos that they can share. One day, I would love to have my entire one-hundred-person team meet up for a couple of days in one of my happy places, Costa Rica.

We're quite happy with the company's size today, and all the leaders feel comfortable with the current headcount, so I don't think we need to get any bigger. Obviously, if we landed a big contract tomorrow that needed twenty-five more people, we'd figure it out, but now we're focused on developing the team we have and improving their skill sets so that all one hundred of them are fully engaged in the conscious connector movement we're building, as well as their own inner work and healing. I want them to be happier human beings in and out of work. That's my primary focus as a leader, but the hardest thing I've ever had to do was learn how to loosen my grip on the company, step away, and give myself space. I learned to be supportive of my team, but cutting myself the same slack was much more difficult.

Creating Boundaries for Someone Who Never Had Boundaries

There I was, trying to do all this inner work while turning the company around during the tail end of the pandemic, but the relationship we had with our biggest client was loaded with friction and completely misaligned with where I wanted to be personally and where we wanted to take the company. My mental health was suffering, and I couldn't sacrifice my sanity and well-being any longer, but it felt like my hands were tied because we had a history with this client and went back a long way.

In the early days of DotConnect, we built the entire team for them. It felt like a start-up incubator, so we were involved in every little decision, and it far exceeded the scope of work we were responsible for. I said yes to things I shouldn't have, and it snowballed. The floodgates were open. We were having meetings and then fifty different sidebar meetings and setting a bunch of calls to discuss what was really going on in those meetings because nobody could come right out and say it the first time. They would Slack us and message us and, if they wanted to vent, call us to yell about candidates at all hours. I learned many lessons from working with them around the clock. Their culture was cutthroat, and everyone was jockeying for position, so working with them became highly inefficient.

I had been sucked into this toxic leadership dance at a time when I was trying to purge the toxicity, but what I could I do? COVID-19 was still an issue, and they were our biggest client, so most of our team worked with them. I was focused on finding other work and getting us out of that situation, but there wasn't a lot of other work out there, and we didn't have much money coming in. I decided to forgo my own journey for the sake of the company to keep the client happy, and my team paid, but I couldn't do it anymore.

I made a declaration to Angie that things would change. I knew I needed to set boundaries with clients but had been putting it off, mainly because I didn't know how. This situation was the straw that broke the camel's back. I needed to step into my power, even if it jeopardized our relationship with this client. I had made my peace and accepted any possible repercussions. I wasn't scared anymore, but before I could act on it and lay down the law, the universe must have been in divine alignment because it intervened on my behalf.

In one fell swoop, almost overnight, the client restructured and eliminated nearly all its executive team. The 280 people we helped them bring in over the previous three years—gone. Their roles were eliminated. One of the toughest clients of our lives had been removed from our world … just like that. I suddenly looked at things differently. All those little details we sweated and were traumatized by, and that had slowly chipped away at our souls, didn't matter anymore.

None of it was necessary after all. I had missed moments with my team, my family, and my friends. So. Many. Times. And guess what? I can't remember 99 percent of what was discussed on those calls that pulled me away from what I was doing at the time. What I do remember are the moments I missed. The times when I was with my son while Gulli made dinner and I stepped away. The times I was out with friends and had to leave the room to take a call. The list goes on and on and on. I wasn't going to make that mistake ever again.

> *I can't remember 99 percent of what was discussed on those calls that pulled me away from what I was doing at the time. What I do remember are the moments I missed.*

When I first spoke with the new stakeholder hired by the client, I opened up to him about what had been going on for the past three years. I told them flat-out: "You are our client, but I'm also running my own company. I can't be involved in every meeting, participate in every extracurricular activity, and build core programs for your internal teams. I'm not an employee. I'm a consultant who runs a consulting business you work with."

I clearly laid down the boundaries for what we as a company were willing to do going forward if we continued to partner with them. I boiled it down to these four simple bullet points.

- Vendor will organize and manage all stages of the search process from candidate screening to offer.

- Vendor will manage postoffer candidate check-in to help ensure the candidate ultimately joins the company.

- Vendor will maintain contact with new hires following employee orientation to ensure a smooth introduction to the company and successful placement in their role.

- Vendor will provide full-cycle recruiting support for candidates to be placed in other companies in which the company owns equity or shares.

I clarified that we were not responsible for anything outside of that scope. I was waiting for some kind of pushback, but none came. He was perfectly fine with it all! He had no idea what had been happening and took ownership of their role in the problem. It was during that transparent conversation that I could redefine my position and ultimately take my power back. It was all the evidence I needed to reinforce the value of fun and not to take the job too seriously.

Timing-wise, it was fate, but it was also a light bulb moment. I had gone above and beyond for that client as if there was a light at the end of the tunnel. I thought that if I only did a little bit more, I would be in the clear and could pull back, but that was an illusion.

The goalposts will always move if you let them. There is no end to the tunnel. There will always be more to do, and the more of it you do, the more is asked of you. The goalposts will always move if you let them, and you will play that game indefinitely, but when you lay down the rules, stand your ground, take your power back, and they're OK with everything, that changes your perspective and helps you redefine your worth. That was a powerful lesson for both my team and me.

I had never laid down boundaries with clients before. I had made myself available 24-7 so that when clients called, I answered. And I answered immediately, often feeling like the person on the other end of that phone was about to unleash hell on me for whatever did or didn't happen. Old me was like, "Let's talk right now and hash it out." And as expected, we'd each be in our emotions, super-unconscious, and say a bunch of things we didn't mean that didn't solve anything and that almost always required another call to resolve anyway.

New me didn't pick up the phone on the first ring anymore. Sometimes new me didn't pick up the phone at all and let it go to voice mail. There were times when I saw those numbers pop up on my phone that I was dying to answer. Sometimes I'd give in, but I got better at fighting the urge. When I did, I'd later check the voice mail, expecting to hear the drama of the day, but more often than not, it was not an issue that needed my immediate attention. I can now look back and see how so many things I would get sucked into and riled up about often figured themselves out in time. Think of how many emails you're cc'd on in a given week that you don't need to weigh in on or even see. And when people did have issues and wanted to lay into me or my team, I learned to give them time to cool off before we connected. It proved to be better for everyone.

First was the phone; next was the calendar. I gave myself cutoff times. I didn't schedule any meetings in the evening. I started logging out at six o'clock and didn't open my computer on weekends. I admit that was hard, but slowly I started freeing up space in my calendar. That came with guilt in the beginning. Sometimes I'd panic because it felt like there was always something I could or should be doing, but it went deeper than that. Call it fear, wanting to prove myself, or maybe a little bit of both, but I wanted to be ingrained in the company. I wanted to be needed. Overperforming and the need for validation date back to childhood. I felt I had to go above and beyond and be a top performer to prove I was worthy of being loved. That's hard to shake, so when I recently returned from a trip to Peru on a

Sunday, I opened my calendar on Monday morning to see it packed with meetings and calls. *Fuck, why didn't I just give myself a day to reacclimate? Why couldn't I show myself a little bit of self-love?* But the fact that I can recognize that and be aware of what I'm doing allows me to change that behavior.

I'm still far from perfect, but I've come a long way. And the deeper I've gone into my inner work, the more aligned I've become to my personal value of time freedom. I knew I had finally made progress when I woke up one Sunday morning and felt triggered that a client had emailed me so early. For once, I was the one to recognize someone else for having no boundaries. Granted, I was the one who had checked my email, but there was something about it that felt icky—a glimpse into the way I used to be.

One of my assistants once told me that she had never worked with an executive who agreed to have their brain picked when asked more than I. I no longer view that as a compliment. If anything, the workaholic mentality was a crutch that I used as an excuse when I gained weight, wasn't sleeping well, or drank more than I should have, but I created all that myself. And if I created it, I could change it.

I've since learned to embrace the empty calendar. Today, I love having an entire day to meditate, exercise, have lunch with my friends, pick up my kid from school, and just putter around the house if I want. I know that I can see a few meetings on my calendar and decide to move them to the end of the week because they aren't critical or even important. I can focus on what's most important to the company and me. That brings me peace and tranquility and is much better than being stuck on Zoom and playing corporate politics.

Sometimes, I can't help flipping back through my calendar a year or two to see what I was doing. It's shocking to see my schedule packed from morning to night without a minute of free time to myself, but that's what life was like as a control freak who needed to have everything run through me. Looking at my schedule from a few years earlier is visual proof of the damage that can be done when you can't set boundaries and say no. Two or three years ago, I wouldn't even recognize myself today, but I've finally learned how to embrace my value of time freedom. That's empowering, and it feels like an enormous weight has been lifted from my shoulders.

But I've finally learned how to embrace my value of time freedom. That's empowering.

I know the sacrifices I made early in my career did bear fruit. It wasn't all rotten. It has gotten me far. I can reflect on my accomplishments and see what I'm capable of because I invested in myself and bet on my ability, but how I did it was unhealthy and made me miserable. I know that I'm on the right path today when I can sit back and watch my business continue to grow while I set boundaries, live my values, and loosen my grip on the company. That makes me want to continue on that path of healing because it benefits me, my team, and my business, but there was one more step that I needed to take before I could genuinely honor my true, authentic self.

CHAPTER 10

Work Dom versus Home Dom

L ike most people, I've learned how to be different people in different situations. As many of you probably know, feeling like you're always wearing a mask is fucking exhausting. From the moment I started my career at seventeen, I was conditioned to be professional and polished. I had to shed my Southern California attitude, or whatever you want to call it, and everything from what to wear to what to say was drilled into my head. Mentors would edit my emails, not just for grammar, but I would get notes like, "You called this person a 'chick,' and that's not appropriate." Somewhere along the line, I lost my sense of humor and put together a list of what I needed to say and do to be taken seriously. I'm not exaggerating—I really did make a list.

After twenty years of working with over four hundred companies, I figured out how I'm *supposed* to act and what I'm *supposed* to say. I learned how to deal with all the drama, bureaucracy, and politics that emerge daily—even in the tiniest of places—but it was all a facade. It was an act, and I was playing a role that was not in line with the real me. I didn't even realize it was happening because it became routine.

During one team-building event that I hosted at my New Jersey house, everyone was sharing stories, opening up, being vulnerable, and crying when I caught myself stepping away to take a client call. I could feel the switch flip inside me as I transitioned from my authentic self to my work self in a matter of seconds. When I talked to my clients and executives, I knew that wasn't the real me. I would go from being in the zone with my team to being silly at home and suddenly turn all serious and try to be perfect when I got on these calls. It was like I was a different person with a different vocabulary, different standards, and different personalities, giving off completely different energy. And I didn't like it. Something about it felt so phony—if not to the client, then to me. Every time, it chipped away a little piece of my soul.

I know this is something we all do to some degree in various circumstances, and even though it might be challenging to recognize in ourselves, we can spot when other people do it. *Posturing* is a term you might recognize. I'd often meet with clients in a work setting, and they'd be all buttoned up and "corporate." Afterward, I'd catch them at a happy hour, where they would be totally different. "Oh, there you are! There's actually a normal person in there." In the meeting, they acted like *that*, but now they act like *this*. Just give me *this!* I don't want "meeting you." I want "real you," but I couldn't complain because I was doing the same damn thing.

Those closest to me who knew me best saw how I really was, and they were my biggest fans. Why couldn't I be with clients the way I was with them? Why couldn't I call up an executive or hiring manager and be like, "Dude, come on! Let me just level with you." I didn't want to speak in corporate jargon and subtext anymore. I wanted to drop the facade and be able to tell someone they're being an asshole if that's what I felt. No hard feelings … we'd just hash it out. If things were getting too serious, I wanted to be able to make a joke to bring some levity to the situation. It all goes back to not everything having to be so serious. As my coach Cameron says: "Work is just what we do to make money. Chill out."

There was Work Dom and Home Dom. I just wanted there to be one authentic Dom. As I watched everyone jockeying for their jobs, I reached a point where I couldn't keep up with the polished posturing and the consult-speak. I didn't have the energy to keep up appearances. I was exhausted and just wanted to be me, so I made a change. From that moment forward, I tried to show up as my authentic self in every possible situation.

I was exhausted and just wanted to be me, so I made a change. From that moment forward, I tried to show up as my authentic self in every possible situation.

It took some trial and error, but I've managed to find a balance. I was recently on the phone with a client who happened to be an old friend. My team didn't feel valued by a manager on his internal team, so I just told him what I needed. This conversation didn't have to happen in a formal setting. I didn't have to be politically correct or dance around the real issue because I was worried that we'd get fired. I was up front and honest and spoke from my heart. And guess what? There were no hard feelings and no drama. "I'll handle it," he told me. Not only did he compliment our team and the work we're doing, but he also extended our contract for another year. Oh my God! I want all my interactions to be like that!

*Work on closing the gap between who the world
thinks you are and who you know you are. Your
mental health will change significantly.*
—BRIANNA WIEST

This whole journey I've been on for the last two and half years has led me right back to my own heart, and it's made my professional interactions exponentially more efficient. I am able to get right to the point and not worry about all the obligatory formalities and clichéd song and dance. When trust has already been built, you get on the phone, get what you need done, and get off the phone. Boom, boom, boom, boom!

The ancillary benefit was that when I embraced that part of home me that was not always present at work, it became the part of me that many clients liked. Obviously, I haven't done away with all formalities, basic decency, and politeness. That's not that point. But when talking with people I've worked with for a long time, there is no need to sugarcoat anything or pretend I'm someone I'm not. This is how I am. This is how I communicate. And when you show people that you're comfortable being your authentic self, it creates an invitation for them to drop the facade and show up as their authentic selves.

When I recently talked to one of my stakeholders, we took a couple of minutes to catch up, discuss the market, and get into the specifics of our project, and we were done in under ten minutes. "Great! Talk to you next month," he told me. *Wow!* When dealing with the previous person in that role, getting that information and moving the needle would have required multiple calls over multiple days because there was often internal corporate drama on their team. When you work with good, normal, like-minded people who share the same values, life is so much easier. Unfortunately, that's not always possible.

I can't always have it the way I want, and I can't pick and choose the people I interact and work with. Not everyone will be on board with the authentic me or what I'm trying to do. People will only meet you where they are. In those situations, I've started leveraging the Clearing Model, which is an effective nonviolent communication tool I learned from the Conscious Leadership Group.

When things finally came to a head with a client seven months into a yearlong engagement, I used this model to resolve the situation. We had a big team of recruiters working with a client and had already made a couple of hundred hires, but it wasn't an easy process. Our team had to follow a structured, manual process with many steps and disparate systems. That left a lot of room for human error. Miss one thing, and it would all get messed up. There was a lot to remember, and our young recruiters panicked when the client pointed out all these little mistakes.

I had known the client's head of recruiting for over twenty years. He was a peer, so I wanted to resolve the situation and find out whether they were unhappy with us, but it took me weeks to get that call on the calendar. When we finally spoke, I followed the Clearing Model. I started the conversation by thanking him for his time and telling him that our relationship was important. I then asked if he was open to hearing feedback. When you begin a conversation like this, you're getting consent to continue to the next step. It also helps disarm people so that they aren't so defensive. That simple approach sets the tone for a different experience.

I then laid out what our team had accomplished while explaining the challenges we had with their process. I explained how my team was scared for their jobs because they felt they were being micromanaged and demeaned. It didn't seem like our contribution was valued, so I asked if he would rather work with another company. Before I could get much further, he stopped me: "Wait a second. Can we unpack this?"

He then proceeded to tell me that he thought we were doing an amazing job and apologized for giving us that impression. He hadn't heard any complaints from his team, and if he ever had, he wouldn't have let it fester because he would have called me so that we could deal with it together. That one conversation debunked the story I had been telling myself for months. It's amazing how your mind can play tricks on you and get you to believe things that aren't true—things that are almost always worse than they really are.

> *It's amazing how your mind can play tricks on you and get you to believe things that aren't true—things that are almost always worse than they really are.*

The Clearing Model approach helped us alleviate tension and discuss the problems without getting into a confrontation. It also shed light on the reality of the situation that I couldn't clearly see. I've used the Clearing Model professionally and in my personal life to build deeper relationships. And because I've been preaching it to my friends and team, they will sometimes come to me with their own Clearing Model scripts for me to look over before they have difficult conversations. I wish I had known of this tool back in my toxic days because it was a big awakening.

In the real world, not every situation resolves itself this easily. In those cases, I don't place the burden on my team. I step up and work through the issues with our clients to create a win for everyone. If that's what I need to do to improve the working relationship for my team with a particular client, that's what I'll do. And if it doesn't work, and we're forced into a situation in which we must compromise our values, we're in a comfortable enough place right now where that isn't worth it, and we can cut ties. It's that simple.

CHAPTER 11

A New Vision for the Future

When I first started working in the corporate world, my goal was to rise through the ranks and be a senior-level recruiter making great money. At one point, I wanted to retire at forty. I don't even really know what I meant by that, but I think I just wanted to make enough money not to work a corporate job. I wanted what everyone wants—freedom: the freedom to live anywhere in the world; do what I want, when I want, with whom I want; and call my own shots. Making money and enjoying it became the motivation; it was all about the status symbols. That's why I bought the house in New Jersey: that was my way of letting people know that I was successful and smart, had my shit together, and was great at what I did, but it was never enough. It was always about trying to get more—more money, a nicer house, a better car, and more shit. That was my fix, so

I was never satisfied. I could work until I was one hundred years old and never get what I wanted.

When the pandemic hit, my first instinct was to work on my business. In addition to working with Angie and joining masterminds with like-minded business owners, I considered returning to school and getting my MBA. A part of me always wanted to get my MBA from Wharton (because everything I did had to be the best). I loved school, and I loved learning—in a past life, I must have been a teacher. Getting my MBA would mean taking two years and spending $200,000, which would have made sense if I was early in my career or trying to transition into private equity or investment banking, but I didn't need it for what I wanted to do and where I wanted to take my business. So I started looking at alternate routes, if for nothing else than to provide a distraction from the chaos of the world.

I had been a huge fan of Seth Godin for a long time. If you don't know Seth Godin, he's an author, entrepreneur, and business and marketing guru. His writing resonated with me, and he launched an intense monthlong leadership and personal development program called altMBA. I thought it could help me acquire helpful tools to grow my business. I certainly had the time, so I signed up in April 2020 for a cohort that began in July 2020.

I went into this course looking for an authentic academic experience akin to a traditional MBA. I was excited to prove myself, do my best work, and earn an A-plus, but on day one, Seth set the tone when saying that everyone starts with an A. That deflated me a little bit, but the idea was that we were all winning and coming into this on relatively the same level, so this would be the type of course in which you got out what you put in. What followed was intense and totally different from an actual school experience but was something that helped to restore my faith in humanity at a time when I most needed to feel a connection.

There were about one hundred people in the class, and we were divided into four teams of twenty-five. Each week, these groups rotated, so we worked with different people throughout the program. We met every Tuesday, Thursday, and Sunday. We were given a couple of journal prompts every week that allowed us to write about topics such as business, marketing, and sales, but we had to tackle them from a personal and emotional perspective that forced us to go deep and share from the depths of our souls. We would then receive feedback that made us reflect on what we had written and often rethink our views. By the end of the week, I sometimes had a completely different perspective than I did at the beginning.

The course was a challenge but a much different experience than I would have gotten in business school and one that allowed me to reconnect with my passion for writing. Growing up, I was a closet creative until I was about sixteen. I wrote stories, poems, love letters, and anything I could think of, but that all stopped after I broke up with my first real boyfriend. It felt like I stuffed that part of me into a bottle and corked the lid, so nothing inside could get out into the real world ever again. After getting that feedback on my "nonbusiness writing" in altMBA, I felt confident again to take the cork out of that bottle and let the world see what was inside.

During that month, I worked closely with people from around the world and formed bonds with many of them. It didn't matter if they were in New Jersey, Australia, or Germany; we were all in this together and going through the same struggle. We showed up for our Zoom calls on time, ready to unpack all our shit and challenge each other. For a little while each week, we could forget about being depressed and the world coming apart at the seams. I walked away from that experience with a hundred new friends from all over the globe. The benefit proved to be much more personal than professional—or so I thought.

Every time I sought to improve my business or advance my career, I was redirected back to the inner work I needed to do. For the longest time, I looked at them as two different things. I would do the inner work and then work on my business, but I didn't realize that the personal and professional were the same. They are intertwined and can't be decoupled. The personal work I was doing proved to be the most valuable and unexpected professional resource I could have ever acquired because it prepared me for these difficult times when I needed to be physically grounded and present.

I didn't realize that the personal and professional were the same. They are intertwined and can't be decoupled.

In the summer of 2022, every time I logged onto LinkedIn, all I read about were people being laid off and recruiting teams being let go. It was a bad time for our industry. The market had started to shift, much like it had at the beginning of the pandemic. We were dealing with a struggling economy, inflation, and the war in Ukraine. That impacted how companies hired their talent. Business slowed down.

I had been there before, but this time was different because I knew how to better manage my team and repurpose their skills. When things got difficult and I began to doubt or get down on myself (yes, it still does happen because I can get lonely at times and feel unsure that I'm doing the right thing), I didn't crawl into bed and throw the covers over my head. I stayed the course. I remained present and committed to my morning practice and exercise routine. I didn't surround myself with negativity, which meant not consuming media, catastrophizing, or fearing everything that could go wrong. I became very particular about what I let into my field so that I could focus instead on the positive.

More important than anything else, I chose not to react and leaned heavily on the faith I had been cultivating through this inner work. I continued to follow my deep sense of knowing. If I was rattled, I wouldn't be able to focus on my team, and it would only be a matter of time before they absorbed that energy. Panic will sink ships. So when I heard chatter within my team, I got out in front of it. I called a company town hall to explain what was going on and assure everyone we would be OK, even if that meant the company might look slightly different. We had an honest conversation about the state of the company and their future with it. Nobody could control what was going on out there. The only thing we could control was the quality of our work. If they did that, I would take care of the rest.

That was my third economic downturn in recruiting. I learned that things always look different on the other side, and we've always made it out. Every. Single. Time. This time around, I was much better prepared to lead my team through, and it's not because of anything I could have learned from a business book or even directly from another person. I could have only discovered it by going deep within myself. I didn't know it at the time, but working on myself was the best way I could improve my business because it allowed me to gain a healthy new perspective.

Working on myself was the best way I could improve my business because it allowed me to gain a healthy new perspective.

When I think about DotConnect and where we want to be in the future or where I want to be in my career so many years from now, I'm using a completely different metric than I did before I started this journey. It's not about profit or status; the goal is to learn more about myself, help grow my team, and not sacrifice my mental health or well-being to do so. I fill up my cup today through the impacts and opportunities I create for others. Very little lights me up inside like knowing I played a role in someone else's success or hearing the clients endorse our team members and voice their satisfaction.

> *Our team members have brought about this transformation in the culture. They're curious people doing the inner work necessary to bring consciousness to corporate.*

I know what we're doing is working because I can see the results in my team's performance and overall job satisfaction. Externally with clients, our teams don't turn over much. Our people are committed to the work because they are committed to DotConnect and its vision. We can work the way we want without compromising our values, and when a partnership doesn't align with our vision, we have the freedom to decide not to work with that client.

It's no longer just about me, and I'm not the only one who drives change through the organization. Our team members have brought about this transformation in the culture. They're curious people doing the inner work necessary to bring consciousness to corporate. They have become the change they want to see in the world.

Find meaning and joy in the work you do, not the work you wish you did. Finding fulfillment in work is never about pursuing your idea of what your "purpose" is. It is always about infusing purpose into whatever it is you already do.
—BRIANNA WIEST

PART III
Love

Unconditional Love

My grandmother was my champion.

Dorothy Constance Vigil was born on July 7, 1935, one of fifteen children. She was born with a hole in her heart, and after surviving multiple open-heart surgeries, she was told that she should never have kids. She didn't listen. Married at the age of twenty, she went on to mother seven children, the last of whom she was pregnant with when a drunk driver tragically killed my grandfather during what was supposed to be a quick trip to the library on Sunday morning.

Family was everything to my Gram. She lived in a little one-story yellow house with all my aunts and uncles. A few blocks away was the church. My grandmother was a devout Catholic, and she loved attending Spanish Mass on Sundays, even though she didn't speak Spanish. A year before I was born, my dad had lost his younger brother, Dominic. Both he and my grandma had taken it hard, and when I was born, they named me Dominique after my late uncle. I was told that I brought some light back into my grandmother's life, so she poured everything into me and became closely involved in my life when I was very young.

At four years old, I would spend hours with my grandma, hopping on and off the MTA bus in Norwalk, California. While we ventured to the library, McDonald's, Thrifty's for ice cream, and Lakeland Road Park, she would tell me about my grandpa, who she said loved me and was waiting for us in heaven. She spoke about him as if he were alive and talked about how one day, we would all be together as a family.

Gram watched me at her house one week when I was sick and had to stay home from school. Even though I started to feel better by the end of the week, I didn't want to leave, and Gram didn't want me to leave, either, so she called my mom and told her that she'd watch me another day because I was too sick to go back home. She hung up the phone and winked at me. We just wanted to spend one more day hanging out together on the front porch. I was close to her in ways that I couldn't get close to my mom or dad because she wasn't a parent. In my grandmother's mind, I could almost do no wrong, so our relationship didn't have any friction. She always accepted my path and what I wanted to do in ways my parents couldn't.

My grandma was my best friend. Maybe I was an old soul or she a young soul. Call it twin souls or kindred spirits, but our connection was rare. She was my reason for being. In my mind, she is the epitome of unconditional love. She didn't only have love for friends and family; she also showed acceptance, support, and warmth to everyone she met. Talk to anyone who knew her, and they'd say the same thing. Love just poured out of her, and it was contagious. It didn't matter whether I was having a good or bad day, whether I was celebrating something or pissed off … she was always my go-to person. Because of that, I constantly tried to impress her and make her proud.

In the '70s, Gram had survived breast cancer and undergone a mastectomy, which was a brutal, traumatizing experience back then, but she recovered. When I was seventeen, I learned that the cancer had returned and begun to spread. When my dad broke the news to me, he could barely get the words out. He was hysterical. His eyes were bloodshot from crying. It was difficult to see this macho six-foot-four 220-pound guy so distraught. My mom was in Europe, so I spent the night on my parents' couch because my dad didn't want to be alone. I was in shock and couldn't wrap my head around the fact that my grandmother had cancer. *She was in her sixties. She was young and seemed so healthy, happy, and energetic. She went to church. She was the perfect person. How did this happen?*

I wasn't the only one. The next day, the entire family sprang into action. All my aunts and uncles came together because the thought of losing Gram was something none of us were ready to accept. My aunt put her on a vegan raw food and juice diet. They tried all kinds of natural remedies to slow down the cancer so that they didn't have to resort to chemo and radiation. And it worked. We didn't lose my grandmother that year or the next. She continued to be my biggest supporter, my best friend, and my rock. We talked all the time, and I told her everything. I loved talking to my grandmother because she didn't have to say anything. She just had to listen, and often that's all she did. Later, I'd get a letter, and that's when she'd give me advice. I'm glad I recently found those letters because I still look at them today, and they continue to be sources of inspiration.

I was twenty-four when her health took a turn. I came home one weekend to visit, and when I picked her up to go to lunch, I noticed how sickly she looked. She wasn't herself—she was all skin and bones. That was hard for me. My initial reaction was to yell at my parents for not taking care of her. I didn't realize that they had been, but her situation had deteriorated. She went into the hospital soon afterward, and we all knew her time was limited. On the day she died, I held her hand and told her everything would be OK.

After Gram passed away, the doctor said he was surprised she didn't complain about being in more pain because the cancer had spread to her bones. I think she was in tremendous pain but suffered in silence because she didn't want the family to worry. I think she also knew that if she had spoken up or told the doctor how she felt, they would find something and want to do more treatment, so she decided to ride it out. I believe she knew she wouldn't make it out when she went into the hospital.

As a family, we didn't know what to do without Gram. She was the matriarch—the nucleus who held everyone together. Without that presence, it was difficult for us to express love to each other in the same way. Something was missing, and everything suddenly felt cold. Slowly, everyone drifted apart.

I felt particularly lost and confused, as if I didn't know who would pour love into me the way she had. Something was frightening about her absence because I didn't have anything to fill the void she had left. That was the first significant loss in my life. I tried writing her letters, but even those turned out angry because I couldn't imagine how any God would let something like this happen. At that point in my life, I had a very different perspective on death and transitioning.

My grandmother may be gone, but I still feel her energy and use that as a source of strength. When meditating during a recent psilocybin ceremony, I saw my grandma and asked her if she was proud of me. She said, "I've always been proud of you, and I always will be. Stop trying to impress me and live your life."

Even today, my grandmother continues to teach me about love. My definition of love has transformed over the years, but today I believe the word that best encapsulates love is "acceptance." It's being able to meet your partner, children, friends, colleagues, family members, and even strangers with no conditions. That's how my grandmother lived her life.

> *Today I believe the word that best encapsulates love is "acceptance." It's being able to meet your partner, children, friends, colleagues, family members, and even strangers with no conditions.*

When I was younger, love to me was conditional and situational. I'd think of it like, "If you look like this, I'll date you." "If you wear that, I'll date you." "If you stay thin, I'll date you." It was an emotional and irrational feeling that quickly came and went. I didn't realize that I was only scratching the surface of what true love really meant. I'm sure some of that was hormonal, but things tended to get volatile when love went wrong in my world. I've since learned that you can't truly love anyone else before you learn to love yourself. That was a problem because I was so highly critical of myself. That's something I've been working incredibly hard on since the start of my journey, and I do that by trying to tap into that maternal side that I inherited from my grandmother and practice unconditional love. I don't know if I will ever be able to love the way she did, but I try.

Love is a word I say frequently, but I mean it when I say it. I say it to my friends after every conversation and phone call, but love isn't only about what you say; it's also about what you do. My grandma encouraged me to reach for a high bar, and even though I now realize that I sometimes set the bar a little too high for myself, I've learned how to gently encourage those around me to do the same. That means supporting the people around me on their own journeys so that they can step into their strengths and absolutely always meeting them where they are with acceptance and without any conditions.

At the end of the day, all we really want are a few close people who know us (and love us), no matter what.
—**BRIANNA WIEST**

CHAPTER 13

The Give and Take of
True Partnership

I moved to Newport Beach when I was sixteen. That's when I
started taking some early college courses, and it's also when I
met my first boyfriend.

I was at the beach with a group of friends when Chris
walked up and introduced himself. It turned out he was my neighbor.
It also turned out that he had a girlfriend, but that didn't faze me. I
told my mom that I had just met the man I was going to marry. Chris
and I became friends and grew closer when his girlfriend moved to
Los Angeles, and his relationship fizzled. By the time I was eighteen,
Chris and I were inseparable. I used to pour my heart out to him in
love letters I wrote that he then kept in his top dresser drawer, but our
relationship quickly turned rocky.

Chris was older. He could go out to drink at bars, but I couldn't
join. I got so jealous when he landed a job bartending on a boat to
make extra money. The mind games and insecurities I experienced

were a recipe for disaster. One weekend, his mother sat me down and told me that I was too young to be in love and that I should move on with my life because the relationship wouldn't end well. I'll spare you the details, but she was right. Our relationship devolved into disaster.

First love was intense for me. I would call up my mom and grandma in tears, telling them that I didn't know how I could go on with life. I still remember those feelings, and for the longest time, I didn't think I would ever recover, but the mushroom cloud of devastation eventually settled. It took time, but I began to piece my life back together. I learned that no matter how dark and painful the experience, you can make it to the other side of trauma. It might not seem like it when crying yourself to sleep, but if you just keep going, you will get there. However, I believe this

No matter how dark and painful the experience, you can make it to the other side of trauma.

heartbreak left its mark and started the hardening process that transformed my loving heart into a piece of coal. I never wanted to be hurt like that again, so I tried very hard to feel nothing. I just withdrew from any emotional attachments to men after that.

In the following years, I moved out of California and had a few boyfriends, but I felt lonely, so I threw myself into work. Things finally started looking up when I met an Australian executive on a trip back home. He was thirty-eight, I was twenty-three, and we didn't live in the same city, but none of that mattered because I felt that feeling all over again. We met up again a month later, and he paraded me around and introduced me to all his friends. I felt special and wondered if he was "the one." I started planning my future life in Australia. We decided to meet up next in Costa Rica and go to my friend's wedding together. Life was good, and then I got the call. The Australian told me that he was getting back together with his ex and wouldn't be going to the wedding. It turned out this was just a summer fling after all.

I felt sick. I felt used. I felt like an idiot. But this time around, the depression was tolerable. I knew I would be OK, but my heart got just a little bit harder. Worse, I started to feel jaded. I moved back to San Clemente, California. I had a good job and good friends I saw regularly, and I started dating a few local guys but nothing serious.

One night that fall, I got talked into meeting up with an ex-boyfriend and my friend Maya at Javier's in Laguna Beach. While at the bar, I heard Maya make small talk with an Australian guy. My ears immediately perked up, and that's when I met Gulliver. Yes, like *Gulliver's Travels*. He had long, scraggly hair, and he was artsy. I could tell he was different, and when I joined Maya and my ex at a nearby table, I couldn't stop looking at him. Before we left, I wrote my number on a napkin, crumpled it up, stuffed it into his hand, and said, "Call me or I'll kill you." I dropped Maya and my ex off and then went home to bed. Before I fell asleep, I got a text from Gulliver asking if he could take me to dinner. The next day, he texted me some inspirational quote, which he later told me he thought was stupid, but at the time, I needed to be positive and focus on the good, so it helped me more than he realized.

On our second date, we drove up to Los Angeles for dinner. On the drive home, I made a joke, and he had this deep belly laugh. He thought I was funny and laughed at my jokes. When I spent time with Gulliver, I could tell he was different. When we spoke, he looked at me—really looked at me. Once again, I had that feeling, the one I tried very hard not to have, so I wasn't going to come out and say it yet. I wasn't going to get hurt again.

I had been single for a while and was dating different people, but that involved a lot of games and noncommitment. Nobody I dated really wanted to stake their claim and come right out and call me their girlfriend. Nobody until Gulliver. He liked me, and he was honest about it. He was convinced I was his girlfriend after a couple of dates. I had to explain to him how, in America, we dated people and how I was dating people, among whom he was one, but still, he was very forthcoming about wanting me to be his girlfriend. In his mind, that was it. And I knew he was serious when he cut his hair after my dad made a comment about it.

Three months into our relationship, Gulliver and I moved into a condo in Newport Beach with my sister and some friends. We were like a big happy family, and I have some of the best memories of my life in that house, but my career and life were in flux. We also started to fight a lot but never about anything important.

We were young and immature. We both worked a lot and worked for our weekends. We had a ton of friends, so we'd go out to drink and do a lot of partying—Gulli was always the life of the party. That came with a lot of drunk arguments about stupid shit, so for the next five years, we fell into a pattern of breaking up and getting back together every three months. For the longest time, I wanted to control the situation and even him at times. That was just my way of being back then, and it led to a few of those breakups.

In my gut, I always knew that we'd either go our separate ways or get married, but I still had this vision of the picture-perfect family and home life, so I made the decision for us. I chose the latter, and when I was twenty-six, we got married. It was a time when all our friends were getting married, so that created added pressure. Instead of taking the time to ask, "Is this person right for me?" I said, "Fuck it! That's it! I'm not doing this shit anymore. We're getting married." I arranged it all. I got the diamond from my mom's ring; we found a jeweler who made a new ring, and I gave it to Gulliver. "Here's everything. Propose to me when you want, but everything is already lined up, so it's going to happen." Like everything else, I pressured the situation and didn't let it unfold organically.

That approach worked for us, and I have no regrets about any of it, but it was clear from the beginning that the two of us had different views, values, and lifestyles. He was a night owl, and I was an early-to-bed person. He was creative; I was more logical. Despite the differences, we've grown together over the last fifteen years—you can't help it when faced with the challenges of starting a family and losing a home. We've learned what modalities work for us. It may be breathwork and meditation for me and surfing for him, but we've come to accept each other's individual journeys, yet we appreciate our differences in ways we didn't initially. That's eliminated much of the friction. We're each on our own path. Mine may be ten times faster than anyone else's, and sometimes it works out really, really well, but it's not always easy.

There are plenty of times we find ourselves stuck in a circle of resentment. Technically, we've been fighting about the same thing for fifteen years. We even joke about it because we each know that neither of us is ever going to win, but that's just our topic. We've had real conversations about separating and hitting pause. I know there is more that I can do, and part of my healing work is taking responsibility and focusing on becoming the best version of myself so I can be a better partner, but that doesn't always come naturally. What's even more difficult is letting Gulli know that. I may have no problem telling all the other important people in my life that I love them, but my husband is the person I struggle to say it to and with whom my attempts are met with resistance. I know I don't tell him I love him and show him affection when I should. That's because I have a huge fear of rejection or lack of reciprocation when I put myself out there, and that holds me back.

His friends picked up on it the night we first met. They told him not to talk to me because they thought I was too intense and told him to stay away from me. During those times when we're coming from very different places, it feels like we're living life on repeat, and neither of us will ever be happy or fulfilled. Sometimes I've thought about taking a step back, letting go, and just stopping working on our relationship for three or six months and see what happens. Gulli had suggested we attend therapy, and initially, I was a hard no whenever the topic came up, but I did agree to go. I look at some of my friends who have been in therapy for twenty years and are still discussing the same issues from the past. I wasn't comfortable with a mediator in the room while the two of us rehashed old stories and got into who said what. I didn't see how that would fix any of our problems. It's not that I can't learn lessons from the past, but I want to be more forward thinking and work to improve the next phase of our relationship. That's what I think a good coach does. They help you create awareness and take responsibility for your own healing while making sure you're headed in the right direction. It's someone who helps you accomplish specific goals over a shorter period, but this relationship wasn't only about me.

I have a huge fear of rejection or lack of reciprocation when I put myself out there, and that holds me back.

Marriage is about compromise, and you have to be willing to try different shit, which is why I changed my stance on therapy when Gulli asked again. Therapy might do us some good and help us break this weird, murky, and unhealthy impasse we find ourselves in. We'll never know if we don't give it a shot. It's easy to get divorced. It's easy to throw up your hands and say, "I don't want to do this anymore. I'm over it. It's too hard." People do it all the time, even if they know it leaves a trail of destruction behind them. I don't want that to happen to us. I'm invested. We've been together for fifteen years, married for ten, and I don't want to give up that easily. That means I must be willing to have those difficult, often uncomfortable conversations. It means I have to take responsibility for my shit as well. At this point, we are both committed to our own healing journeys so we can be the best possible versions of ourselves—first for ourselves, and then for each other.

I have no idea what the future holds. No matter what happens, I do know that it's been a great, loving relationship that I wouldn't trade for anything in the world. We've grown together and as individuals who love each other deeply. Marriage has taught me a lot about myself and invaluable lessons on patience and acceptance. That, to me, makes ours an incredibly successful relationship, and nothing will ever change that.

Motherhood—The Days Are Long, but the Years Are Short

A year after Gulli and I were married, all our friends who had just gotten married started having kids. That's when I was like, "All right, let's do this!" For some reason, I had it in my head that I wanted a baby before I was thirty. Gulliver may have been ten years older than I, but he wasn't ready and didn't understand the rush. However, I was determined. I wanted my child to grow up with all my friends' kids, so in 2013, Baxter was born.

Once you have a kid, they're there. Having children is not something you get on the bandwagon and do just because your friends are doing it. We don't even hang out anymore with those friends whose kids I wanted my son growing up around. You really need to make sure you're ready. I mean, you're never really ready, but it changes a lot. It's difficult to put into words the change motherhood has made in my life. I look at Baxter and love him so much it physically hurts my body. It's been amazing and simultaneously so difficult. Some days I'm wiped. "Permanently tired for life," or PTFL, is a saying I came up with because sometimes it feels like no matter how much sleep I get, I'm still exhausted. Then, at other times, it's like the complete opposite, and I have this infinite bucket of energy to draw from because I have another person to care for. I'm still astounded by that and have no idea where that energy comes from.

It's difficult to put into words the change motherhood has made in my life. I look at Baxter and love him so much it physically hurts my body. It's been amazing and simultaneously so difficult.

Up until Baxter was born, it was Gulli and I who did everything together. We had a lot of time for ourselves, but with a child thrown into the equation, it suddenly became all about him. We call him "the Prince," because he's the center of it all, and he knows it.

In the beginning, I didn't feel like a good mother. That's a wound that cut deeply, and I still carry a lot of mom guilt because I focused on work when Baxter was young. I told myself that I had to provide for our future because I was the breadwinner, so I was on the road for long periods. I was also emotionally absent and not fully present during those early years. I missed out on a lot of milestones, and that's something I wanted to change, given my own upbringing. My childhood was stable, but my father wasn't involved much when I was younger. He was a hustler, always trying to make money. He worked really hard, and now that I'm a parent, I can appreciate the desire to provide for a family. That's how my dad was wired, and it's how I'm wired. I understand why my father made the choices he did, but that doesn't mean I have to make the same mistakes or sacrifice being a good mom. I've since learned to take ownership of the fact that our mother-son relationship didn't always look how I would have hoped, but equally important is that I'm learning to release that. I'm forgiving myself and working to be present now. More than anything, I feel so grateful that my beautiful boy loves me.

I'm lucky that I don't have to do any of this alone, and I have a partner who is an amazing parent. Watching how Gulli has leaned into becoming a father to our son has made me fall in love with him on a deeper level. He shows up as the caring and nurturing parent better than I do at times. He has so much patience with Baxter, so I've learned a lot from watching him. And Baxter is all about his dad. In that regard, it feels like I'm playing catch-up. I'm working hard to build my unique relationship with my son, and watching how Gulli shows up as a father has inspired me on my own parenting journey. I still want to make sure that I'm capable of providing and giving my family these amazing opportunities, but I also make sure that I can be with them to share all those beautiful experiences. Balance is required. My friend Lindsay recently changed her priorities from work, kids, relationship, and herself to putting herself first, relationship second, then her kids third, and work forth. I love that, and even though I don't think I'm there yet, it's a place I strive to reach because it's a healthy framework for working parents with kids.

Now that I'm leaning into the role, motherhood has made a difference in me in ways I never thought possible. One thing that's rubbing off on me is that it's helping me be more childlike and fun. I'm generally pretty serious, and Baxter is only eight, so he's silly and always wants to goof off. When I catch myself trying to rein that in, I have to stop and make sure that I'm not turning down the volume on that natural instinct. I don't want my son to be doing all this healing work when he's in his thirties and talking about how he never had a relationship with his mother. I've become very mindful of that, so I want him to feel like he can express himself and just be a kid because it goes by so quickly. It's already going by. I remember Baxter being six months old like it was yesterday.

The role I needed to play as a parent was never more evident than after we lost the house in New Jersey. That was a reminder that we were all in this together. I was depressed at first, then Gulli and then Baxter. The energy would rotate, and it became difficult to coexist those first few months. Baxter grew up in that house. It not only contained all of his belongings but all his childhood memories as well. That void was replaced with a lot of anger. It was so difficult to see our son become someone we didn't recognize, and it never really went away until we got Baxter settled and comfortable with school and friends. We needed to be there to help him through that because that situation wasn't only about us.

Experiences like those are an excellent reminder to me that maybe I should learn how to be a little more connected to my own inner child. Growing up, I was very mature. Looking back, I think of myself as a miniadult in a kid's body. I had a good childhood with good friends and a lot of good memories, but I was always rushing to get to the next phase of my life. At ten years old, I had a calendar that I used to count down the days until I turned sixteen so that I could drive and get a job.

During a recent inner-child meditation on a healing retreat, we did an exercise in which I had to write a letter to my younger self. It felt like I was transported back and came face-to-face with myself at seven. I walked into the house where I had grown up and through the door into my room, where I played Barbies. That child was so excited that she got up and gave me a big hug. I told her, "Don't rush. Take the time just to be a kid. Don't worry so much about being an adult and doing adult things. Enjoy this!"

I see other mothers who can naturally be childlike around their kids, and a part of me wants to be like that. One thing I catch myself doing is not being as soft and nurturing a mother as I should be. I think back to how my grandmother was the most affectionate human being, so I feel so harsh and strict by comparison. I have to remind myself that Baxter is still young, so I can be silly, light, and fun with him. I know I'm being hard on myself because there are some days when I can be that fun, cool mom who cracks jokes, but there are other days that I have my guard up, even with my son.

One thing I'm working hard on is treating myself with more grace. I can see huge improvements in how I've shown up as a wife and mother in the past couple of years. Baxter has told me that my energy has changed and that I'm more present. "You aren't always on your phone" is how he phrased it, but it's encouraging that he can notice a difference. I like the feeling of actually being able to go on vacations and spend time with my family. The other night, Baxter even asked me to do breathwork with him. He's intrigued and inspired, so hopefully, the positive changes I'm making can rub off on him.

I'm changing the way I show up for my son, and I think Baxter has been a tremendous teacher in unconditional love. I'm constantly reminded of this when it comes time for him to go to bed. Like most kids, he argues and puts up a fight, and there is always some kind of drama, but eventually, we get him into bed, and he falls asleep. The next morning, he's up and immediately all sweet and loving and wants to cuddle, as if all the drama from the night before never happened. None of that matters to him anymore, and that's how it goes with kids sometimes. They rebound quickly. A toddler can have a tantrum, and then five minutes later, they want to give you hugs and kisses. It's an emotional roller coaster, but it's such a beautiful thing and a reminder of what's important.

Redefining Friendship

My decision to join Gerard Adams's Conscious Leaders Mastermind in February 2021 would forever change my life for the better.

From the first call with this group, I immediately felt accepted, seen, and acknowledged in ways I hadn't before. And this was from people who didn't know me or my story. They didn't know anything about my dramas. They had just met me and were still so warm, accepting, open and welcoming, without any conditions. They asked me questions that had nothing to do with work—that was refreshing. We didn't discuss money, power, or status, and I realized that I wasn't seeking validation for accomplishments or possessions. These people were genuinely interested in who I was on the inside: why I thought the way I thought and even what I thought about. They took me in with all my scar tissue, sins, and fuck-ups and just loved me for who I was. It was different from any other group of people I've ever met, even among my so-called true friends. And that didn't go away over time.

The next level up from the Conscious Leaders Mastermind is One Infinity, a group I've since joined that Gerard leads with an artist, poet, and coach named Adam Roa. And Adam Roa is pure magic.

I've learned how much the people you surround yourself with can light you up, and very few people light me up like Adam. He has a dynamic vibe and a beautiful mind that make him one of my favorite people. When on coaching calls, he can get into this zone of genius that feels like a pure flow state where everything he says is mind-blowingly profound. When I get off those calls, I'm just buzzing. He's made me think differently about so many things. When writing, I often feel like Adam is looking over my shoulder, providing inspiration to go deeper and truly examine what I'm feeling. A few weeks ago, I had a deep cry about our old house, and I immediately tapped into my "inner Adam" by writing a poem to help process my feelings.

He said, "You're a diamond, and diamonds come from the center of the earth. They have all the pressure in the world on them, but they don't break."

Pharoah Kyle is another one of the leaders I connected with through the mastermind. He read my astrological chart and told me there were certain trials and tribulations I needed to endure, but then he said, "You're a diamond, and diamonds come from the center of the earth. They have all the pressure in the world on them, but they don't break." That resonated with me and was exactly what I needed to hear at that moment. Kyle was just one of the many solid, trustworthy people I met who I know have my back. We all check in with each other just to make sure that we're acting in alignment with our goals and vision for the future. For the first time, it feels like I have people who are not calling me out but lovingly calling me forward.

I tip my hat to Gerard for setting the tone and embodying that level of acceptance. He'll admit that his path was very different. He used to be hard and lived a very different lifestyle until beginning his spiritual journey seven years ago. When learning all these new spiritual practices, I've met so many great, positive people who fill me up. I simply don't have space for people who have a negative or low-vibe energy anymore, but I've learned there is a trade-off.

The sad reality is that the deeper I go on my healing journey, the more I grow apart from some people who used to be close to me. Not everyone I'm close with has to be on the same path as me, but if people possess a particular type of negative energy that I'm trying to remove from my life, I have to set a boundary, wish them well, and move forward. Still, there is always something about the end of a friendship that is sad; it almost feels like someone died. It was difficult for me to cut ties with people at first. A part of me almost felt guilty, but I'm starting to learn that it's OK for friends to grow apart. We

There are many seasons in life where people come and go. Some stick around longer than others, and that's OK.

can learn to appreciate the friendship we once shared, respect each other's differences, and go our separate ways. Just because we were friends once, that doesn't mean either of us is under any obligation to continue that friendship. We all must follow our own paths, and there are many seasons in life where people come and go. Some stick around longer than others, and that's OK.

It's one thing to grow apart from someone you have no ill will toward, but it's another to have a falling-out with drama. I'm also learning there is a healthy way to grow apart from someone you've had conflict with, and I haven't always adhered to that. For a very long time, I was a grudge holder. If I ever felt wronged about anything, I would carry that resentment and energy with me for a very long time.

I recently attended a retreat with Anahata Ananda, who taught us that instead of meeting conflict with conflict, we should meet it with curiosity. She drew a cyclone and used that as an example for how easily other people can pull you into this vortex of negative drama and suck you down. It happens so easily because our natural reaction is to meet that conflict by getting defensive, which is meeting conflict with conflict. That locks the two of you in this downward spiral that sends you straight to the bottom, so instead, try meeting conflict with curiosity. Tell yourself, *Maybe there is something here for me to learn.*

For the longest time, my instinct was to meet conflict with conflict, even when it wasn't necessary. A close friend and one of the first people I hired at DotConnect comes to mind. We worked together for a long time, and I used to call her one of the OGs because we all thought she would stay with us forever. She made it through COVID-19, and when businesses started ramping up in 2021, she was working on many different projects. One day, she burned out, snapped, and quit.

I felt really hurt because after all we'd been through, she could have come to me first. She could have told me what was going on and how she was feeling. I would have supported her and come up with solutions. She could have even taken a break. She didn't need to quit. It surprised me because I thought we had a much deeper connection. I'd always support one of my team members if they felt there was a better opportunity elsewhere, but that's not what happened. I wished her well, but I was so hurt and sad that I just drew a line in the sand and cut ties in my head.

I didn't hear from her for a while. Then, she reached out a handful of times and sent me text messages about what was going on in my life, but I didn't have much to say back. I was still holding onto that disappointment, and as far as I was concerned, that chapter of my life was over. Then, for a while, I forgot about it. A few months later, after I moved back to Laguna, I had a dream about her in which we had a very specific conversation that laid out everything we had to say on the table. I woke up and realized that I did miss her, and she had been a good friend. We had a genuine relationship, and my ego had prevented us from burying the hatchet. I didn't realize that I had been holding onto that negative energy. Even though I wasn't thinking about her, that energy was still inside, and it was toxic. I had to let that shit go, so I texted her. It turned out that she was moving back to California, and we'd be neighbors.

We recently reconnected and met in person. Releasing that energy felt good. It also made me realize that I had missed her and wanted her back in my life.

Cutting ties with those who have a destructive energy and not holding grudges with those who I feel wronged me were not things I set out to change—it all just kind of happened naturally. It was a by-product of the inner work I had been doing. When you take the time to be more self-aware and start looking inside, it becomes obvious how much energy you're wasting on all these different forms of negativity that just don't matter. We stay angry for no other reason than because that's the story we've been telling ourselves, and it's playing on repeat in the backs of our

We stay angry for no other reason than because that's the story we've been telling ourselves, and it's playing on repeat in the backs of our minds.

minds. We don't realize how much easier life can be when we choose to release that negativity. That doesn't necessarily mean that we have to sever those relationships. It's more about learning how to be open and honest, even with yourself.

One of the biggest lessons I've recently learned about friendships is that they shouldn't be difficult. My relationships with my best friends and those closest to me are not hard at all. They've never been hard. When I look at my relationship with Erica, my COO and one of my best friends, we've never had any real issues that came between us. We don't fight or argue. That doesn't mean we see eye to eye on everything, but we support each other's differences and support each other's healing journeys. I have other friends whom I've been through a lot of shit with, and there were periods where we had to take a break from each other and didn't speak because there was so much drama. That's not healthy.

Imagine if for every person you met, you thought of some way to help them, something you could do for them? And you looked at it in a way that entirely benefited them and not you. The cumulative effect this would have over time would be profound: You'd learn a great deal by solving diverse problems. You'd develop a reputation for being indispensable. You'd have countless new relationships. You'd have an enormous bank of favors to call upon down the road. That's what the canvas strategy is about—helping yourself by helping others.
—RYAN HOLLADAY

Relationships are a two-way street, so I'm also starting to pay more attention to how I show up as a friend because I know that I've shown up differently throughout the years. I'm used to being the leader who makes all the plans and rallies everyone together. Before moving to New Jersey, I felt almost like the party mom. I wasn't nearly as conscious then and was more interested in superficial fun, but even that ran its course, and eventually, work took over. That's when I became the friend who was always back at the house or locked in the hotel room making phone calls while everyone else was out having fun. There was a close group of friends whom I used to travel with to Nantucket every year, and we'd rent this gorgeous place, but after three years of me working the entire trip, they stopped inviting me. Nobody wanted to be around me anymore while trying to have fun on vacation, and I don't blame them.

Healthy friendships are about give and take, but the trick is finding balance. I never had any problem being there and giving to others, but as a control freak who insisted on doing everything herself, I sometimes struggled with the taking. One way that manifested was in my inability to ask for help from others when needed, but I like to believe that is changing as well. I can't do everything myself, and I shouldn't try.

When we made the move from New Jersey back to California after the flood, I was reminded of the importance of having close friends. When we lost everything, we had to start over, and there was so much work to do. At the end of an eighty-hour workweek, the last thing I wanted to do was search for a house so we could start a new life. It was overwhelming. It was difficult to stay on top of laundry and other chores, so all that stupid shit piled up and became a source of tension in the house. I needed help, and I admitted it for the first time ever. It took a disaster before I began to ask for help. It started with my uncle, who volunteered to help load up all our stuff into a U-Haul and drive it cross-country. Our friends stepped up until we got settled. I could lean on them and, much to my surprise, found comfort in that. We started hanging out with my dad's big-ass family. I had them over for meals, barbecues, and holidays. It felt like I had stepped back into my grandmother's matriarchal role for a while. Once we found our place and settled in, I began to outsource tasks that did not bring me joy or were not in my genius zone. That was difficult because I was in a scarcity mindset, thinking I didn't want to pay for anyone to help me do things I could do myself.

Accepting that I am not good at everything is something I need to embrace if I'm ever going to fulfill my personal value of time freedom.

It's new for me, but I'm not ashamed or embarrassed to ask for help or speak up when I need something anymore. That's big, coming from a recovering perfectionist and control freak, but accepting that I am not good at everything is something I need to embrace if I'm ever going to fulfill my personal value of time freedom. To do that, I had to be vulnerable enough to relinquish control and trust others. Not everything will be done my way, but that's perfectly OK.

I saw just how far I have come when my mom and sister planned a surprise birthday party for me in our new house in 2021. They invited everyone—members of my team and even best friends from childhood. It was quite impressive because normally they can't get anything past me, but somehow, they pulled it off. And I had a great time, which is also strange because I'm not a surprise party person. I'm the planner. I'm the one who organizes the surprise party, so it was odd to be on the receiving end and not the one in control calling the shots, but I really did have a great time. It's all about learning how to let go and embrace this new role. I don't have to be the way I was before or buy into that story I had been telling myself for so long.

Today, I make it a point to keep my circle small and intentional. I have many acquaintances and an extensive network of colleagues and clients whom I could easily put in the friend bucket, but I don't feel obligated to make that commitment anymore. I'm at a point in life where I want to only spend time with those who are an energetic match or give back what I can pour in. I want to be friends with people who show up for me the same way I show up for them. It's nice to have a smaller group of conscious friends where it's not always about drinking, partying, going out, and spending money as much as it is dropping into conversations and connecting over interesting things. It's about supporting each other through the ebbs and flows of life.

CHAPTER 16

Giving Back

Until recently, most of the trips I took were with my girl-friends. They turned into boozy and bougie vacations where we set out to relax and have a good time. I still make time to take those trips whenever possible, but my perspective on what a good time entails, where to go, and what to do when traveling has started to shift.

In 2019, I traveled to Necker Island, which is Richard Branson's own private island in the British Virgin Islands, with an Australian women's networking and career community called Business Chicks. That was the first year I was running DotConnect, so it was a great networking opportunity for me. I wanted to be around this group of women who had bigger businesses, achieved more success, and had all of this abundance, prosperity, and impact. It felt like they were playing a different game on a different level, and I wanted to learn what I could from this group of powerful badass women to help me level-up my game.

One component of the trip was to help a group of women raise money to build a domestic violence shelter in the British Virgin Islands. They already had a daytime facility where women and children could go to be safe during the day, but they didn't have many sleeping areas or overnight housing. That was important because if you're a victim in an abusive relationship who decides to leave, you need to have a safe place to stay.

Many of these brave women shared their gut-wrenching stories about not only surviving horrific instances of domestic violence but also even going to jail for fighting back against their abusers. These were violent and sometimes deadly situations in which these women found no escape. Since getting out of jail, they have been working to help other women.

I didn't know much about domestic violence before meeting this group, but the statistics were heartbreaking and alarming. What stood out to me, and what I had never realized before, was the reason why women remained in these abusive relationships. Every situation is unique and has its own set of challenges, but such a large percentage of women stay because they don't feel like they have any options. Many don't have the training, experience, skills, or opportunities to go out on their own to earn the money they need to support themselves or their children. They feel stuck, so they stay.

That's when I thought of my grandma. She wasn't a victim of domestic violence. Her challenge was much different. She always wanted a career but never had the opportunity because she was left to care for her children. When I was young, she told me how she dreamed about going out into the world to make an income for herself and doing something that made a difference. It wasn't until she was sixty-five that she found a job at the Honey Baked Ham store in her small hometown when she finally made a little bit of money for herself. She was someone who wanted to learn a skill so that it could create an opportunity, but she never had that chance.

The eye-opening stories these women told and my grandma's dilemma came together at that moment. That's when a light bulb went off for me. I can do my job remotely from anywhere in the world, including the BVI, where they were trying to build these shelters. What if I could teach these women skills that would help them create more opportunities? I wanted to leverage whatever I could to help. That's when I got the idea to start a nonprofit. I would consider it a master class in which I teach my craft and corporate business so that these women could learn the skills required to begin generating income. They might not have the résumés, but if we could teach them the skills, they could then go out and get jobs. That would help them break the destructive cycle and take back their power.

When I returned home after that trip, I reached out to some domestic violence shelters to begin discussing the project and how DotConnect could contribute. It's quickly become a cause that is near and dear to my heart, but that was only the beginning. When I met Gerard and his group of successful businesspeople and conscious leaders, the idea of giving back and being of service moved to the forefront of my brain.

Our first trip together as a group was to Tulum, Mexico, in April 2021. After two months in the mastermind, this was my first chance to meet all of these wonderful people in person whom I had only talked to online. We stayed in this beautiful villa, where we ate great meals and did all our healing work, but that wasn't the only reason we were there.

Tulum is so beautiful, but the area just outside of Tulum is super-violent. There are drugs, cartels, violence, and corruption. It's just not the safest area, so it made sense that a conscious leader's mastermind would look to use our resources to create impact and be of service to the people in those communities who needed the most help—the children.

As a way to give back to the local community hosting us, we spent a day working with kids at a childcare center. These kids, whose parents worked in the area, didn't have a school to go to, so they went to a center that had been built on a rundown block of land. I didn't speak Spanish, and they didn't speak English, but we played, laughed, painted, and had a lot of fun the entire day.

> *I have more than most, but what am I doing with it? How am I giving back?*

That experience day put a lot of things in perspective. I am very lucky. I have more than most, but what am I doing with it? How am I giving back? Seeing how even the simplest acts of kindness could light up these kids made me redefine how I thought of true wealth in my life. That thinking becomes infectious.

> *Let yourself be drawn by the stronger*
> *pull of that which you truly love.*
> —RUMI

A similar experience occurred in April 2022, when I traveled to Peru with the same mastermind, and we volunteered at a local school in a rundown area. During our stay, one teacher and her ten students showed up late. We later learned that the teacher had to travel an hour and a half up the Amazon River a few times a week to teach these kids. We were able to spend some time with her, and after hearing her story, I felt inspired. If anybody deserved a little help, it was her, so I decided to sponsor her school. We donated money to buy school supplies, toys, and even basic necessities like shoes.

I'm still dedicated to my company. As we grow and thrive, it creates more opportunities for us to make a significant impact through acts of service and volunteer efforts. These experiences also serve as reminders of what I need to be grateful for, while putting many struggles and troubles in perspective. If I can leverage just a little bit of the abundance that I've created to help impact other people, especially children who need a helping hand and exposure to knowledge necessary to make better lives for themselves, I will jump at that opportunity. I believe that ties into

Success means nothing if you can't show up and be of service in the communities where you are and impact their people. That's another, and perhaps the most impactful, form of unconditional love.

what it means to be a conscious leader. Success means nothing if you can't show up and be of service in the communities where you are and impact their people. That's another, and perhaps the most impactful, form of unconditional love.

PART IV
Wake

CHAPTER 17

The Evolution of My Spirituality

My grandma was Catholic, so I grew up attending a Catholic church. I was never baptized or considered myself a practicing Catholic, but I'd still go with her to Mass every week. As I got older and learned more about religion, I thought God was some dude with a long beard and white robe in heaven. I wanted to distance myself from that. I never thought about it much, but I had a one-track mind and considered religion and spirituality the same thing. And because I wasn't religious, by default, I didn't consider myself spiritual, but I wasn't completely devoid of spirituality.

A few months after Gram's death, I was so distraught that I moved back into my parents' house. When they were away, I slept in their room. During that time, I was in a deep depression and couldn't work, so I wouldn't get out of bed. One afternoon, I heard a raven tapping on the outside of the window. All. Day. Long. I didn't want to get up, but this went on for hours and annoyed me so much that I finally went to the living room and looked up. The raven was sitting right there on the windowsill in the skylight. It wouldn't move; it just sat there and stared at me. I don't know what made me think about it, but I felt my grandma's energy—her presence—in that bird, and she was trying to get my ass out of bed. "OK, Grandma, I got it!"

I knew that I couldn't lie in bed all day. I had to get up, get my shit together, and do something. So I took action and called my therapist. I was finally ready to get some help processing my grief. I had to accept that grief wasn't something I would get over—I had to learn how to integrate it with my existence. They say that your level of grief is equal to your ability to love, and that resonated with me because losing my Gram was a significant loss to which nothing in my life has ever compared. After that moment, I was a little more at peace.

That wasn't the only time something like that happened. There were times when I could still feel what I believed to be her energy. It's difficult to articulate precisely what I felt, but I sensed she was sometimes there with me. What I later came to realize was that I felt closest to her during moments when I committed to myself. So when I was exercising and doing healthy things, I would feel very connected to her, but when I wasn't or stuck in a negative space, I didn't. You're either suppressing your feelings or feeling your feelings, so the more I was present and in my body, the more spiritual I felt, even if I wasn't yet sure what any of that meant.

After the pandemic hit and my life devolved into chaos, I was definitely not committed to myself. I was drinking and had run myself ragged; my business was in jeopardy, and my marriage was falling apart. That took every ounce of feeling I had about anything and pushed it deep down inside, so I didn't feel anything. I was lost and at my lowest. I told Angie that I don't feel connected at all to my grandma like I used to. *Where are you? How do I connect with you again? What the hell?* I was so lonely because it felt like I didn't have that spiritual guidance.

Since I was a kid, the ocean would reset my nervous system. Looking out at the vast horizon that appears to have no end calms my soul. I was living in New Jersey then, so I drove out to Montauk and rented a house. That presence came back as soon as I went out on the beach. Maybe it was my grandma, or maybe it was just being out by the ocean, but I felt spiritually connected again. I was slowly developing a new understanding of that energy.

In January 2021, Angie gave me the book *The Power of Now*, by Eckhart Toole. In the beginning, he explained how he would reference and share learnings from all different spiritual leaders and religions. He gave readers permission to identify with them or not, but the idea was to extract what we could from the lessons. That intrigued me. It got me thinking that I could be more open and still find value in certain religious or spiritual purposes without having to buy into any religious dogma that I still had an aversion to. It opened my eyes and made me realize that spirituality could be whatever I made it out to be. Something inside shifted, and I set out to create my own spiritual practice to serve as my energetic personal connection with the universe.

I had learned transcendental meditation twelve years earlier, but it never really stuck. Meditation actually made me more anxious. I struggled to get relaxed enough to drop in and be present. My mind raced, thinking of everything I had to do and the places I had to go. It was all consuming, so I could never commit to making meditation a habit, especially when my calendar was booked for sixteen hours a day. I used to power through my day without any breaks, so sitting still proved difficult, if not impossible, but breathwork resonated with me in ways I could not have expected.

During that April 2021 trip to Tulum with Gerard and the conscious leaders' mastermind, I was introduced to Miriam Adler, an amazing practitioner who taught us holotropic breathwork. I can't help but feel that it was all divine timing. I wasn't even going to attend that trip at first. It was on the cusp of the twelfth anniversary of my grandma passing away. It was also during the pandemic before the vaccine was available, so people weren't traveling much, but I changed my mind and booked my ticket at the last minute.

Before we began our first breathwork session, Miriam explained that when doing it right, breathwork can be like taking LSD. Just by the way you breathe, you can trigger certain parts of your brain that are activated when taking psychedelics. I had never done LSD, so a part of me panicked. *Hell no! I don't want to do this!* I was scared because I had no idea what would come up, but I had no frame of reference either. Despite my fears, I gave myself permission to try it.

There were about thirty-three people in the group, and we all lay down while Miriam gave simple instructions: take two breaths in, hold, exhale. Ten minutes in, I was overcome with this beautiful feeling. It felt like my body was short-circuiting, almost like I was dead and was going to heaven. I felt myself being pulled and lured toward something. When I got there, I saw my grandma as a beautiful blue raven. The visual was sharp, as she took me underneath her feathers, where I felt safe. She told me to pull all my family members close so they could be healed. There was a straightforward message that I wanted to carry back to my family to let them know that Gram was OK. She also told me that I needed to forgive my dad because he had done the best he could, and his pain wasn't mine to carry anymore. I knew that she would always be around and that I could always tap into that healing energy, but it was my turn to take the matriarchal torch and carry it forward for all of us.

When I came down after that session, I started crying my eyes out. The whole thing was crazy, so I had to sit with that feeling and figure out what the hell had just happened. At first, I was groggy, but then I felt much lighter because my body had just released all that fear, anxiety, and pain I had suppressed.

I looked around, and everyone's reaction was different. Some people cried as I had. Some screamed. Some were making fists and punching the air. Others felt nothing. It was such an individual and unique experience, but for many, I believe they got more than they anticipated. I know I did. I felt so much gratitude being in my grandma's presence and was finally at peace with her no longer being with us. I knew that was why I came on that trip, and I was right where I needed to be. I felt a sense of closure and no longer feared that my grandma was in this dark place. It felt more like a version of heaven, or whatever you want to call it, and a place that I one day hoped to visit. Had I not experienced that, I would probably still feel lost and in mourning, but breathwork shifted my perspective and brought me closer to my spiritual side.

We do not "get over" a death. We learn to carry the grief and integrate the loss in our lives. In our hearts, we carry those who have died. We grieve and we love. We remember.
—NATHALIE HIMMELRICH

You can do certain types of breathwork during meditation, and the practices can certainly overlap, but I found this specific type of holotropic breathwork to be much more impactful and healing than meditation. It's more of a mind opener for me that acts almost like a magnet to pull all that negative emotion that I've been carrying around out of me. And once it's out, it's gone, and I don't have to carry it around anymore. That's so liberating. The best way to describe the effects is to compare it to an exposed nerve ending. When you have a toothache, you're hyperalert and aware of sensations and anything approaching that pain point. And this journey takes you through a wide range of vivid and intense emotions. Each one bubbles to the surface, where it sits, allowing you to dig through and observe what has been buried for so long. The experience can be intense and knock you out for the rest of the day, but the emotions that emerge can linger for a long time. You can spend days unpacking what surfaced.

That experience changed my perspective, and I started making breathwork a regular component of my spiritual practice. Today, I'll do three-minute mini breathwork sessions a few days a week to help keep me centered. Some of the longer ones can last an hour and are not always as intense or heavy as that first experience. Sometimes I can take in the beauty all around me. I often have this vivid visual of me, my grandma, my grandpa, and Uncle Nick all floating on the water with our arms outstretched and connected to form a star. We're all so calm and peaceful that it creates a sense of bliss inside me. These experiences are often very visual, like doing psychedelics, but it all happens by controlling the breath.

I'm so grateful for being turned on to breathwork because it's changed my life and has been a massive catalyst for much of my healing work that followed.

I'm so grateful for being turned on to breathwork because it's changed my life and has been a massive catalyst for much of my healing work that followed. It opened the door and allowed me to walk into rooms I never thought I would enter. More than anything else, I'm grateful for it helping me better connect with my grandma. I now connect with her when I'm in a calm, peaceful state, and breathwork is one of the best modalities for that communication. I have zero other thoughts in my head, so I can deeply tap into that energy.

I've learned that connection with my grandma also comes through during my writing as well. She used to write a lot, and I was reminded of that when I found that collection of letters and writings in our garage. I'm lucky to have moved that box out of the garage and upstairs to my office before the flood. As I read and reflect on what she's written, I've started writing her back. And even though praying was never my thing, I sometimes find myself in the morning setting intentions and saying my version of a daily devotional prayer where I open up and try to tap into my grandma's presence. Throughout the day, I often get signs that draw my attention to her energy and let me know she's still here. I can't help but think that's what's happening whenever a bird comes up close to me. We could be anywhere, and these big, beautiful birds always seem to fly up next to me. It happened recently at the beach when I was just sitting there. I like to believe that energy is my grandmother. Maybe it is, or maybe it isn't, but thinking that brings me peace.

CHAPTER 18

Venturing into the World
of Plant Medicine

Verlin was a member of our conscious leaders' master-mind. She was this crazy intelligent quantum scientist who became a close friend. When in Tulum, I told her about some of the issues I was having in my relationship. That's when she introduced me to plant medicine, which are plant-based psychedelics, such as ayahuasca, psilocybin, and dozens of other plants used in healing ceremonies all over the world for centuries. It's not like any of these are grown in a lab—they are all natural and come from the earth. Different plants provide different experiences; not all are available or legal in the United States. Ayahuasca, for example, is illegal in this country, so people often travel down to South America, where the plant is grown. They make the medicine right from the vine before conducting the ceremony.

As she described this, it all sounded so foreign to me, but it was also intriguing. I had minimal experience with psychedelics. I had done mushrooms once recreationally when I was twenty-six and in Amsterdam with Gulli. It was a horrible experience. We got into a massive fight, and I told myself I would never do anything like that again, so it was definitely not on my radar. I'm a control freak who wasn't comfortable letting go or disassociating with my thoughts and identity, but things had changed.

Psychedelics can be taboo for those who aren't already involved in this consciousness realm. It's often misunderstood, but there's a big difference between doing psychedelics recreationally and using them for healing purposes. It's become a therapeutic way for some people to take action to treat depression, anxiety, and PTSD. There's a bit of a renaissance going on with psychedelics, even in corporate. After research and studies by several universities and nonprofits, they are slowly becoming more acceptable. When I was in Vegas for a conference, there was a panel on psychedelic therapy that attempted to destigmatize the experience and teach it as a healing modality. Many have found it a more effective and more natural alternative to the pharmaceuticals that some doctors can push on their patients. I discuss this topic with Angie and those close to me in my inner circle, but I don't post about it often. When I do, I'm always surprised by how many former clients and executives who reach out and share their own experiences with psychedelics.

For a long time, I lived with depression and anxiety. I was high functioning, so I never identified it for what it really was or admitted to myself that I was suffering. My marriage wasn't in a good place, I was growing bitter, and there was a lot of dark energy inside that I didn't realize I was carrying or know how to get rid of. I felt a strong calling to shake things up, so when I returned from Tulum, I asked Gulli what he thought about traveling to Costa Rica to participate in a healing plant medicine ceremony with another couple. We had tried everything else. I figured we were on our last leg, so we could either split up or try this deeply serious healing experience to see what came of it. He agreed.

Participating in a plant medicine ceremony is not something you ever want to take lightly or go into without preparing or educating yourself. It's also important to mention that plant medicine is absolutely not for everyone, so I'm not recommending it if you aren't ready or don't feel comfortable or safe. My friend Lindsay was a hard no on plant medicine, and I respect that, but after she educated herself about it, she joined a mastermind with me, and we traveled together to Peru. If you are interested in learning more, I recommend the series *Psychedelica,* which is eight episodes and available on Gaia. It's an excellent introduction that does a deep dive into so many different plants. *How to Change Your Mind* is another great Netflix documentary hosted by Michael Pollen. The more I learned about the intelligence of these plants, the more reverence I developed for the entire experience.

This was a big step for me and seemed completely out of character, and the only reason I agreed was that I knew Yerlin would make me feel safe. I loved her energy, and I trusted her. She was 100 percent the person I wanted to guide us through that first experience. Having done my homework, I knew how important it was to have someone with you whom you love and trust and who has good energy because there is always the chance that emotions come up that you may not know how to deal with. When that happens, you want that person there.

When we showed up at this beautiful house overlooking the ocean, I had no idea what to expect going in. Gulli had done psychedelics before, so he was like a pro, but when we sat down and started setting our intentions for the session, he was much more nervous than I. I wasn't nervous at all and was ready to dive right in. By that point, I felt ready to go deeper. I was curious, and I knew I needed to remove all that baggage eating me up inside so that I could ascend to my next level.

I knew I needed to remove all that baggage eating me up inside so that I could ascend to my next level.

I was prepared for the experience to be impactful, but I wasn't prepared to be completely rocked the way I was. Shortly after taking this medicine, I saw my sixteen-year-old self and started crying because I missed that beautiful soul. Where had she gone for the past twenty years? I could see how every trauma had slowly chipped away at her without me even realizing the damage it was doing. What followed was hours and hours of crying. It was a lot. The experience was intense for both of us, but it exposed the healing work we didn't even realize we needed to do by revealing all that baggage we had carried with us from childhood into adulthood. It explained why we were the way we were with each other in our relationship.

After that experience, Gulli and I felt much lighter and had completely different energy for the rest of the week. We felt grateful to be there and started connecting on a deeper level. We were more playful and bonded friendship-wise in a way that we hadn't since we first started dating. That took a lot of the pressure off us and changed the dynamic of our connection. It made me want to be better, do things differently, and show up more lovingly.

What's beautiful about working with plant medicine is that you're creating neuroplasticity in the brain. You're creating new neural pathways and space in your prefrontal cortex. If your habits and thought patterns are like well-worn tracks through the snow, this experience makes it easier to get off the beaten path and take a new one. Plant medicine isn't the only way to create these new pathways, but it's been a way that many people have opened up their minds and learned that it's possible to change.

A month later, I participated in another group plant medicine session in Costa Rica. I actually feel like they were too close together because that first session was such a deep, expansive emotional purge. I felt good after the first one—I felt complete. So during the second experience, I intended to hold space and contribute to the collective energy. I didn't want to cry or purge. I focused on just pure love and light. I wanted something peaceful, but there was a completely different energy this time around. I was part of a larger group, some of whom had never done it before. Once we began, I could see that a few in the group were nervous. It quickly became chaotic! I felt a bit anxious, but I decided right there to not get pulled into anyone else's energy or experience. I would stay in my lane and hold onto my peace, love, and light. I couldn't control what anyone else would do, so I wished them well, hoped they had a good experience, and focused my energy on something positive. And it worked. No crying, nothing. I remained calm, and even though no heavy emotions came up for me during this experience, I still had an incredible journey.

For me, plant medicine proved to be such a mind-opening and expansive healing modality that helped me tap into my innermost essence. It felt like I could disassociate with my physical body to connect with my true soul, spirit, and a deeper level of conscious-ness. The three terms that best encapsulate this experience for me are *humbling*, *profound*, and *life changing* because the medicine can show you your blind spots. It exposes the things you might convince yourself aren't there or aren't an issue, but if left to stew and aren't confronted, they can easily drag you down. Plant medicine certainly isn't the only way to achieve this state or level of understanding, but it proved to be a powerful wake-up call for me.

This spiritual aspect of my healing journey started with breath-work a year and a half earlier and continued through these plant medicine experiences to form a massive arc that took me to where I am today. It's amazing how much healing has occurred just from these modalities. They've helped me relinquish control and realize that I don't need to carry the weight of the world on my shoulders. They have helped me be more open and not let fear control me and everything I do. They have helped me approach the future with an open mind. It was one of the most beautiful things I've ever experienced, and it couldn't have come at a more appropriate time because the pandemic made it clear how very little we can control in this world. That's difficult for someone like me to accept because I want to be in control of everything. These spiritual experiences have helped me realize that the only true thing we are in control of is how we respond and choose to show up. I can choose to be a victim, or I can choose to be grounded and peaceful in my being. Which one is going to help me deal with everything going on around me?

> *I can choose to be a victim, or I can choose to be grounded and peaceful in my being. Which one is going to help me deal with everything going on around me?*

At the end of the day, I want to keep an open mind with no expectations and be able to live life on a high frequency with peaceful love and light. I'm not scared of the future. I'm open to whatever happens, and I will go with it.

Sometimes you have to kind of die inside in order to rise from your own ashes and believe in yourself and love yourself to become a new person.
—GERARD WAY

CHAPTER 19

Big T and Little T

The more I made breathwork a regular practice, the more I found myself stirring up feelings about my childhood, specifically about my father. He worked a lot, and I always felt like I had to try hard to be acknowledged by him. I think we have the same type of personality, which can be good and bad. It's good because I have drive and can hustle to make money from nothing to become successful and provide for the family. I get that from him, but it comes at the cost of not always being present. I struggle to find joy in the little things and always think about what's on the horizon. Like my dad, I often come from a place of scarcity instead of abundance. And honestly, neither of us is all that fun. Now that he's retired, he's living his best life, but during my childhood, he was a grouchy old-school UPS driver who became bitter because he hated his job. He wasn't always fuzzy and nice, and it felt like I had to tiptoe around him sometimes. Whatever the cause of these feelings, they had been on my mind, and I had been carrying around a lot of resentment and anger from childhood. There were definitely some deep wounds, and I was expecting that's what I was going to purge during my next plant medicine session when I traveled to the Peruvian jungle in early 2022 with a mastermind.

We had planned another series of plant medicine sessions, this time with ayahuasca. We went out into the middle of the jungle, where there was a lodge over the river. This place had no electricity, so we had no choice but to sit and listen to the sounds of the jungle. You could hear everything, which made the experience all the more potent, but it didn't unfold as expected.

None of the feelings I had recently felt about my dad came to the surface, but what bubbled up instead was my relationship with men. Every single guy who had a significant impact on my life must have appeared, but they weren't just romantic connections, so there were men from my professional life who also appeared. It was like their faces were projected on a movie screen, and I started to relieve these experiences with boyfriends, bosses, and everyone in between. I could see and feel all the trauma I had carried with me from these relationships and experiences—many were the results of just being a female working in male-dominated environments. I hadn't thought about some of these things in years, but I still carried them in my body. These relationships were heavy—some downright exhausting. It made me realize how much energy this had depleted from my essence and was probably one of the reasons why I couldn't show up as lovingly in my marriage as I would have liked. There was obviously some kind of trauma around men that I had to work through, but I was reluctant to go down that path at the moment. That resistance made the experience extremely difficult and painful.

Right there in that lodge, I got sick and reached a point where I couldn't throw up anymore, but my stomach hurt, and my body was still trying to purge. I was choking and couldn't breathe. I tried to get up and go to the bathroom, but I collapsed and physically couldn't move. The entire lower half of my body ached. At one moment, I saw five different shamans standing over me, praying and chanting. I was gasping for air and thought I was going to die right there in the jungle. I was done. I just wanted it all to go away, but even through all of that, I still felt safe and supported. I continued to say my mantras: "I'm safe. I'm loved. I'm here."

My problem was that I had been trying to control my experience. As a control freak, I can't help but think I'm more powerful than I really am. I'm always trying to predict outcomes, and it can be difficult for me to just go with the flow, but the ayahuasca was in charge and would be until I let it do what it came there to do. That's when I lay down and surrendered. I gave up control. Suddenly, I felt lighter and had new energy. For the rest of the journey, I pictured myself lying in my grandma's lap while she rubbed my head. It was beautiful and felt like a rebirth. All that came through from there on out was love and compassion. That demon or whatever was inside of me was gone. And then, poof! It was over. Nothing came up about my dad. Maybe those scars are healed. Maybe it wasn't the right time, and I needed to get that other emotion out of my body first.

What plant medicine does better than anything else I've ever experienced is rid the body of trauma.

I know this experience can sound intense, scary, or confusing to anyone who hasn't been there and done it. Why fly eight hours to do this? I get it, but it's tough to describe. Sometimes you must go through hell and get all that shit out of your body to be absolved. I felt grateful to heal instead of having to carry around that burden. In a few hours, the ayahuasca got to the core of what would have taken ten years of therapy to achieve. I left it all out there in the jungle and did not have to bring any of it back to the States with me.

What plant medicine does better than anything else I've ever experienced is rid the body of trauma. *Trauma* was a word I rarely ever used about anything I experienced because I never considered myself to be traumatized. It wasn't until I started doing breathwork and then experiencing the plant medicine that all of these feelings, memories, and emotions that I had suppressed for so long emerged. And much of it could be traced back to childhood. Something as harmless and ordinary as overhearing my swim coach talking shit about me to my mom was trauma that set off a chain reaction that turned me into a hyperachieving perfectionist. Who knows? I might have grown into a normal fucking kid had I not experienced that. All of those experiences were trauma. My grandmother's death, my first heartbreak, feeling belittled as a woman in a male environment, my relationship issues, the arguments, the breakups, losing our New Jersey house, and all the things that led to me hitting rock bottom during the pandemic were traumas that my body stored like stagnant negative energy.

I know the word "trauma" can trigger some people, especially those in my family. My mom once said, "You're posting a lot about this so-called trauma. What happened to you that's so bad? You make it sound like you've had this horrible life."

Not all trauma is created equal. There is Big *T* trauma and Little *T* trauma. Big *T* trauma is exactly what it sounds like—violence, war, rape, and the severe injury that can occur during an attack or a car accident and can be more intense and acute. We're still learning about the effects of trauma on the brain, but it's often physically painful and leaves mental scarring just as damaging as what's on the outside. I'm grateful that I haven't ever experienced that type of trauma. However, I have experienced plenty of Little *T* trauma that created wounds I carried with me for a very long time that never healed. I'm not alone. We have all experienced Little *T* trauma, no matter how good our upbringing or how perfect our lives look on the outside. Trauma includes all the microaggressions and emotionally painful moments in life that you've tolerated and were never able to let go of. You can pretend that it didn't happen, but you still carry that around with you in your body just like you would Big *T* trauma. Your lived experience is your lived experience, and whether you refer to it as trauma or not, your brain doesn't necessarily know the difference between Big *T* and Little *T* trauma, so it reacts to each the same way.

> *Your lived experience is your lived experience, and whether you refer to it as trauma or not, your brain doesn't necessarily know the difference between Big T and Little T trauma, so it reacts to each the same way.*

That's something my mother and many others don't understand, but my trauma is my trauma. Whatever it is that happened to me made an impact, even if it's not what someone else considered trauma. I'm the only person who could know that, and nobody else can tell me what is or is not trauma for me because they don't have the same feelings and emotions. I didn't understand this until I went through these experiences and was able to release that trauma from my body. Only once that burden was lifted did I realize the true meaning of the word *trauma*, and that's something new that I only discovered in the past few years.

To heal, you need to rid your body of that toxicity; otherwise, it will linger and become a cancer that eats you alive from the inside. You have to be willing to look into the depths of your soul, be curious about what's down there, and not be afraid of what might come up. I'm not saying that plant medicine, breathwork, or any one modality is the only way to do it. Everyone is different, and there is no one solution that's right for all. The whole point of your journey is to become more self-aware and to learn what works best for you

You must do the work. And when you do, you'll be surprised what you're capable of.

because nobody else can do this healing work for you. You must take ownership of your trauma and its impact on you and whether it's going to seep into other areas of your life. You aren't going to wake up one day and find that it's all gone. You must address it. You must do the work. And when you do, you'll be surprised what you're capable of.

In lieu of letting go of our trauma and rather than healing completely, in my experience, we learn how to carry it and there are some days when it is heavier than others. Some days, I hardly know it is there, distracted as I am by present joys and excitement; while other days, the burden is cripplingly heavy, and I can hardly breathe under the weight of grief.
—L. M. BROWNING

On our last day in Peru, we set out to hike Machu Picchu. I don't fucking hike, so I hadn't quite thought this through. It didn't help that everyone kept talking about how difficult it would be. I didn't need to hear that after spending five days in the jungle having my mind blown wide open. I was wrecked—tired, fragile, and emotionally fatigued—but I wasn't going to back out either.

We got up at two thirty in the morning so we could be on a bus at three o'clock that took us an hour into the city before hopping on a train for an hour and a half. We finally reached the base of the mountain. When we started hiking, we couldn't even see the top, and every time we turned the corner, we were met with another in an endless series of stairs that kept going straight up. I was miserable when we set out. I kept telling myself how much I hated hiking and didn't want to be there. I'm scared of heights, so I made it a point not to look down because I didn't want to freak out or lose it. At times it felt like I was holding on by a thread, but after a few hours, something inside me changed. The voice in my head started singing a different tune. *Look at you. You're hiking. Hiking is cool. You like to hike. You're a good hiker. Keep hiking.* It felt great to be out in nature, and I even started thinking I should hike more when I got back.

After three hours, I reached the top of that mountain and was so overcome with emotion that I just started crying. I was so proud of myself for doing something I never thought possible. I'm afraid of heights, and I had just climbed this huge-ass mountain with no gear or anything. I couldn't believe it. If I could do that, it felt like I could accomplish anything!

CHAPTER 20

The Road Ahead

L ooking back upon the past two years of this healing journey, it's felt like I've blasted off and gone straight up. I know I'm only just beginning, but I've learned so much and come so far in such a short period. I've also met so many amazing people. They come from different cohorts and different groups worldwide. They may not all know each other, but I can't help but think of them as my community.

The path I followed may not be the best path for everyone. I know that when I get into something, I go all in. There is no such thing as halfway with me, so when I first started out, I wanted to do everything! That meant joining every group and mastermind. Some served their purposes for a short time but ran their courses, and others I knew right away weren't good fits for me. Only about 20 percent of what I tried stuck, and almost always, the X factor was the people and the energy they brought to the table. That energetic match needs to be there for me, and when you have that connection with someone, you know they will be there for you in the long haul. What's so great about all the wonderful people I've met along the way, from Angie to Gerard to Lindsay to Adam Roa, is that they are all so very different and fill me up in different ways. However, that connection is rare, and it might take a while to find your people, which is why you want to have patience.

I'm often approached about joining various masterminds, but I'm more particular now about whom I spend my time with and what groups I join because I'm also a significant contributor. It's not only about what other people and groups can give me. I absolutely love being a superconnector who brings people together. I've always embraced being the person who amplifies my friends and shares everything that has helped me in the world. That's changed how I view any potential new groups, and at this point, I better understand my bandwidth and know that I can't do it all, so I need to be selective.

If you're just starting this journey, know that it's about quality, not quantity.

If you're just starting this journey, know that it's about quality, not quantity. As much as you want to do everything and find all the answers right away, you don't want to bite off more than you can chew. That's why I always tell people that the best first step is to find a coach. That's the first thing I did, and Angie was my foundation for all the growth that continued after that. I'm lucky that she was constant and my rock, without whom I probably wouldn't have felt as free to experiment with so many different modalities and groups as I did. I knew that I always had her support to help ground me if something didn't work out or I feared that I had veered off course. Look at any top-performing athletes or executives, and you'll see that they have coaches, probably a few, and therapists as well, but in my opinion, investing in a coach is the best decision you can ever make for your health and wellness.

I would like to one day expand the conscious culture we've built at DotConnect. I've seen how it's changed my business and life, so I know I can do the same for other people and businesses. We've already gotten interest from clients and other companies about helping train their people so they can build a similar culture. My friend Lindsay and I have discussed creating a mastermind for emerging leaders in the early days of their inner work practice—people who need support to build healthy routines and find their own path. We want to take the lessons we've learned and try to distill them into a three-, six-, or maybe even twelve-month course. The idea is to let people know they don't have to feel like shit. They don't have to continue posturing and be different people at work than at home. It is possible to become authentically aligned in all areas of life and live up to their potential.

I hope to make what I do one day different from those who inspired me by gearing it more toward the corporate space I already play in. I see so many people struggling with the same issues I did. I want to become a more active leader in this realm because I love people and introducing them to experiences that can help them. That's why one Monday

I want to become a more active leader in this realm because I love people and introducing them to experiences that can help them.

morning, I surprised my team with a thirty-minute breathwork session on Zoom. They thought they were attending an all-hands meeting, but instead I introduced them to my friend Avery, who led them through what, for many, was their first-ever session. Some of them were apprehensive, but they went along because, well, how bad could it be?

Afterward, many on the team were shaken to the core just like I was because they had dug up a lot of shit. Some cried. Many messaged me later asking how they could continue this practice on their own. One of the guys had such a profound experience that he quit so he could go back to running his own business full time. That was great for him, and I was fully supportive, but it made me realize that I should think about the timing and be a little more mindful about how these sessions can be received because breathwork is not for everyone. My friend Adam absolutely hates breathwork, and it's his least favorite of all the practices, so I respect that and allow everyone to find their own path and choose their level of involvement.

I've started hosting these monthly breathwork sessions for those who find it helpful. I've opened them up to everyone in my personal and professional network of hiring managers, executives, and clients. I've even had some of the executives who used to yell at me and be my toxic corporate drama people want to do this type of healing because they know they need it. This doesn't just occur in the office. I recently hosted a session at my house and invited a few of my son's friends' moms. It was the first time for many of them, and they had the same experience I did my first time. There was a lot of "Whoa! Holy shit! What the fuck just happened?" It was so beautiful. I can't help but feel good seeing how my journey can influence those close to me to start their own inner work practice. Even when I hear about it after the fact, that little bit of confirmation makes me feel good and reinforces that I'm doing something beneficial for others. I'll screenshot a post and save it in my happy files. Even something as simple as, "I saw you had a coach, so it inspired me to go out and find someone to help me," feels like the ultimate compliment because it means I've encouraged someone to help themselves.

For Thanksgiving weekend in 2021, I brought a breathwork facilitator into my house to host a session with my parents and extended family when they were in town from Colorado. I felt called to help them feel that same connection to Gram as I did. Most everyone took me up on it except for one of my uncles, who was a hard no. I don't know if he was scared when I described my experience, but he was close to my grandma and said he didn't want to go there, which is perfectly fine. The rest of my family, including my parents, were curious enough to go through with it, even though they didn't know what to expect.

Afterward, my mom told me that she wished she had things like that when she was younger. We bonded over that, and I hope it inspired them to begin a similar practice in their own lives. I love being able to help and connect with my parents, but nothing makes me happier than seeing the impact my spiritual practice has had on Gulli. When I started telling him about all these new books I was reading two years earlier, he was annoyed with me. At first, he didn't care about any of it, but slowly he became more intrigued and spiritually conscious. And this is a guy who is a hard-core atheist—no church, no God, nope, nothing, not into it. He didn't even say those words around me, and like I used to, he grouped that together with spirituality. He's *I've come so far, but I also see how much further I have to go.* since started his own practice, and not only have we done plant medicine ceremonies together, but he's also excited to do some of this healing work with me.

I've come so far, but I also see how much further I have to go. I remain curious and open to exploring other modalities. I've been a lifelong learner and have always wanted to learn everything. When our family hosted Thanksgiving when I was a child, I took it upon myself to set up a presentation at the end of the dining room table about the history of that holiday—complete with visual aids. I'm still the same way today (even with the visuals), and I'm excited because there is so much left for me to learn. I recently started working with a neuropsychologist to do brain wave mapping. They hooked me up to electrodes and read my brain waves during a thirty-minute mindful meditation session. I'm not surprised that my brain activity during my supposed "normal state," when my brain was supposed to be relaxed, was all over the place. I still have moments when I experience anxiety, so I want to prioritize this practice and see what I can learn because it would be great if I could truly commit to a meditation practice.

After seeing how much negative emotion and toxic trauma I've been able to purge from my body, and how lighter and more peaceful I feel, I want to see if I can go deeper with my plant medicine practice. I've experimented with microdosing psilocybin—taking very small doses daily while I track how my energy, mood, concentration, and overall level of happiness change over sixty days. I know that it's not for everyone, and I don't recommend anyone ever take that step without being ready and feeling safe, but it's been beneficial in ways that continue to surprise me. These experiences have allowed me to disassociate with myself and visit other realms that have changed how I view life, death, and life after death. Whatever lies on the other side is no longer scary to me. I once believed that I would never be with my grandmother again, and although that may physically be true, my grandmother's energy and presence are stronger than ever. It makes me feel calm and brings me a sense of peace, but that doesn't mean I'm always in that state.

Time freedom is one of my core values, and I've made tremendous strides to free up my schedule. I'm still the face of DotConnect and running my company, but I'm not as involved in the day-to-day anymore. I can now fill my days up with those activities that mean the most to me, but the reality is that sometimes I don't know what to do with myself. My mind starts to race. *What should I be working on? What could I do to get ahead?* One of my primary saboteurs is restlessness. My default is to pack my schedule and charge forward to ensure that I'm supporting my team, adding value to the company, and moving us all toward that shared vision, but I know I need to chill out. I know I'm allowed to rest and not book my schedule, but that doesn't always make it easier.

Sometimes you just need to accept where you are and meet yourself there because when you show up for yourself, commit to honoring your feelings, and put in the work, the odds are in your favor.

The work is never done. Despite the positive strides I've made in the right direction, I still have days when I feel off and can't understand why. Just because I've done all this inner work and learned all of these modalities and tools doesn't mean that I am always the best at using them or that they are magic. Sometimes I get stuck in a rut and can't relax because I'm doom scrolling and getting anxious because I'm doing everything I was taught and still not responding the way I want. *Ugh!*

I can joke about it now because I've learned to give myself some grace and not judge where I am. Sometimes you just need to accept where you are and meet yourself there because when you show up for yourself, commit to honoring your feelings, and put in the work, the odds are in your favor. No negative feeling is permanent. I keep at it because I know that I can wake up the next day, fall into my morning routine, exercise, walk down to the beach, put my feet in the sand, and completely change my energy to get myself back in alignment. I know I have Angie and my conscious leader friends to lean on, and they will check in on me if they notice me being off—just as I do for them.

After doing all this inner work and inhaling, inhaling, and inhaling, I hope to shift into what my friend Adam calls an exhale. I want to take all this new knowledge, combine it with these new experiences and modalities, and get to a place where I can just exhale. That means being able to sit still with all this wisdom and apply what I've learned. It sounds great, but guess what? I'm also starting to realize that this place might not exist. I've watched some of my friends, mentors, coaches, gurus, and people who are all further along on their journeys than I still sit in their shit at times, even when on the outside, it looks like they have it made. That's all just part of the human experience, but just because it doesn't exist doesn't mean that I will stop trying to achieve it.

As a CEO responsible for the financial well-being of one hundred individuals and their families, I don't think I should be able to relax and only worry about myself. I have an emotional obligation. Sure, I could sell the company, retire, and do my own thing. Yes, I have my moments where I get fed up, but I'm not ready to leave it all behind. I feel like I'm living my purpose and doing exactly what I was destined to do in this world. I can't think of anything else I would rather do, so I wouldn't trade this experience—baggage and all—for anything in the world. That doesn't mean I will do it forever, but I know I'm not done yet. It's not time for me to ride off into the sunset. There is more work for me to do, and my role is evolving so that I can make the massive impact I know one day I can make.

What's different now compared to my toxic workaholic days is that there is no plan. I started my company on paper in 2012, but I never intended to run a business. The timing was serendipitous. It just happened out of necessity to have shit organized in 2018. I winged it, which required me to trust my gut, something I wasn't always comfortable with out of the gate. I had hundreds of opinions being fired at me from every direction. I hadn't done any of this before, so impostor syndrome and self-doubt crept in, but the more spiritual I've become, the more I've felt comfortable leaning on my intuition because I'm learning that my instincts rarely lead me astray. It's what has gotten the company and me this far. In the past, I tended to overthink, overanalyze, and try to control the situation; I've since learned to surrender that desire to control and trust my intuition. Even when I'm unable to explain the reasoning behind my decisions to team members, I've earned their trust, so they buy in. So far, my intuition has always been spot-on regarding those types of business decisions, and I continue to receive validating feedback from the universe. I don't need to obsess over and control every little detail anymore. I'm confident that if we do the right things, work hard, and remain true to our values, we will be rewarded for our efforts. I no longer feel like I need a plan. That is incredibly liberating.

As I move forward, I can't help but feel like my grandma has a part in this as well—watching over the company and me. It was her namesake, DotConnect being an ode to my grandma Dottie Constance and me being the recruiter who connects the dots. She could never work the way she wanted when she was on this earth, but look at all the women who now work with me and have learned the skills to create opportunity, wealth, abundance, success, and financial freedom for themselves. We haven't been around that long as a company, but we've grown fast. So much has happened, and I feel like my grandma has been watching my back through it all. Sometimes I feel like I'm only the vessel, and all this energy comes from her.

Today, I strive to live up to my grandmother's example and be a role model for others. I've committed to becoming the best version of myself that I can be, but who am I really? I am also a wife, mother, and business owner. I am a writer, a deep-thinking Enneagram one, and a lifelong learner. I am a reformer, lover, teacher, and humble student of the world who continually strives to be better and to make those around me better by giving more than I accept, practicing forgiveness and gratitude, and loving unconditionally. When you lead with love and remove the conditions, you open the door for deep, real, and true peace.

In the end, just three things matter most: How well did you love? How fully did you live? How deeply did you let go?
—JACK KORNFIELD

ABOUT THE AUTHOR

For over twenty years, Dom Farnan has been a fearless leader in high-growth settings. She blends entrepreneurship and advocacy in all of her roles. Whether she's recruiting talent for titans like Snapchat and Instacart or injecting joy into virtual team meetings through sound and dance, the first thing people notice about Dom is the profound intentionality behind her actions. Always one to see the unlimited potential in another human being, Dom brings radical change to the talent industry through the application of mindfulness, generosity of spirit, and a sense of compassion that values relationship building. Currently, she channels her expertise into DotConnect, the thriving conscious connection agency she founded in 2011.

As a conscious leader, Dom refuses to think in the limiting terms that have been so pervasive in the corporate world. She pulls from her journey of surviving workaholic culture to thriving—shattering the belief that high performance has to cost inner peace. Where others see talent as an end to the means of filling vacancies for clients, Dom sees a holistic picture: bringing talented individuals and dynamic companies together to create inspired, empowering matches.

Just as Dom finds harmony for her clients and their hires, she cultivates it within her own team. She leads with an awakened heart and matches it with unparalleled business savvy. In DotConnect's first year of business, Dom scaled the company to $3 million. From there, Dom's growth mentality has never once subsided. In 2022, DotConnect was honored by being included on the Inc. 5000 list of the fastest-growing private companies in the country. For Dom, the honor is a testament to the resilience and acumen of her team: as the global pandemic ravaged so many industries and slowed hiring, DotConnect grew by 222 percent during that time.

Dom is equally proud of how DotConnect's successes are born from an environment completely cleansed of corporate toxicity—something she and her executive team work to elevate and evolve daily. Dom also Founded DoseConnect. Driven toward future healing and well-being, DoseConnect is a first-of-its-kind talent company solely focused on psychedelic therapeutics. Blending organizational strategy, systems thinking, and talent acquisition grounded in conscious connection, DoseConnect is built to help companies in this space scale for hypergrowth. Working directly with founders, visionaries, and high-level operators, the team at DoseConnect helps companies with everything from human resources systems and compliance to growth culture transformation.

At home in Laguna Beach, California, Dom cherishes creating memories with those she loves and is eager to offer a resounding "yes" to new experiences and opportunities. When she's not spending time with her family, Dom can be found collecting stories, writing, and cultivating her soul-affirming spiritual practice.

Join Dom in her movement toward conscious flourishing:
Instagram: https://www.instagram.com/iamdomfarnan/?hl=en
LinkedIn: https://www.linkedin.com/in/dom-farnan

ACKNOWLEDGMENTS

Mom: Your love of learning inspired me at a young age and instilled a thirst for knowledge. Thank you for fueling my love for teaching.

Dad: Your hustle and work ethic showed me that it doesn't matter where you're from or the cards you're dealt; you can create your own amazing reality.

Gulli: Thank you for always being there for me and our son. Your willingness to join me on this journey is what I've been praying for.

Baxter: You're the reason I took action in my own healing. You are my greatest gift from God. You are my heart.

Ashley: Your support, encouragement, and contribution to our team and me means the world.

Erica: Your belief in me helped create the momentum I needed to keep going, even when I didn't think I could.

Nicola: You planted the seed for me to go all in on myself. Your words of encouragement and support helped launch my company.

Iris: It's always been in the divine plan. Your words of wisdom, insight, and love fill my heart.

Keven: I feel like I've always known you. You inspired me to dream bigger and take a step toward the unknown.

Angie: You are an earth angel, and I thank God for you every day. Your guidance was a light for me when I was in a very dark place, and through that, I was able to find my own light again.

Lindsay: Soul sister, you inspired me to take action on my healing by establishing an inner work practice. I am so grateful for our friendship.

Gerard: My soul brother and superconnector, I am blessed to know you. Your mentorship and support have expanded my life in ways I never thought possible.

Adam: Your magic makes my heart smile. Your mentorship and perspective have challenged me and called me forward, creating space for more expansion.

Yerlin: Soul sister, your energy and support were the tipping point for a whole new world of exploration for me.

1NFINITY: My people. Thank you for being there with me as I went to the depths of my soul to see more of who I truly am.

CPSIA information can be obtained
at www.ICGtesting.com
Printed in the USA
JSHW081933240223
38210JS00002B/7